Best Easy Day Hikes
Albany

Help Us Keep This Guide Up to Date

Every effort has been made by the author and editors to make this guide as accurate and useful as possible. However, many things can change after a guide is published—regulations change, facilities come under new management, and so forth.

We would love to hear from you concerning your experiences with this guide and how you feel it could be improved and kept up to date. While we may not be able to respond to all comments and suggestions, we'll take them to heart, and we'll also make certain to share them with the author. Please send your comments and suggestions to falconeditorial@rowman.com.

Thanks for your input!

Best Easy Day Hikes Series

Best Easy Day Hikes
Albany

Second Edition

Randi Minetor

FALCONGUIDES

ESSEX, CONNECTICUT

An imprint of Globe Pequot, the trade division of
The Rowman & Littlefield Publishing Group, Inc.
4501 Forbes Blvd., Ste. 200
Lanham, MD 20706
www.rowman.com

Falcon and FalconGuides are registered trademarks and Make Adventure Your Story is a trademark of The Rowman & Littlefield Publishing Group, Inc.

Distributed by NATIONAL BOOK NETWORK

Copyright © 2024 The Rowman & Littlefield Publishing Group, Inc.

Cover photos by Nic Minetor.
Maps by The Rowman & Littlefield Publishing Group, Inc.

British Library Cataloguing-in-Publication Information Available

Library of Congress Cataloging-in-Publication Data

Names: Minetor, Randi, author.
Title: Best easy day hikes Albany / Randi Minetor.
Description: Second edition. | Essex, Connecticut : Falcon Guides, 2024.
Identifiers: LCCN 2023057209 (print) | LCCN 2023057210 (ebook) | ISBN 9781493075904 (trade paperback) | ISBN 9781493075911 (epub)
Subjects: LCSH: Hiking—New York (State—Albany Region—Guidebooks. | Trails—New York (State)—Albany Region—Guidebooks. | Albany Region (N.Y)—Guidebooks.
Classification: LCC GV199.42.N652 A436 2024 (print) | LCC GV199.42.N652 (ebook) | DDC 917.47/43—dc23/eng/20231221
LC record available at https://lccn.loc.gov/2023057209
LC ebook record available at https://lccn.loc.gov/2023057210

∞™ The paper used in this publication meets the minimum requirements of American National Standard for Information Sciences—Permanence of Paper for Printed Library Materials, ANSI/NISO Z39.48-1992.

Contents

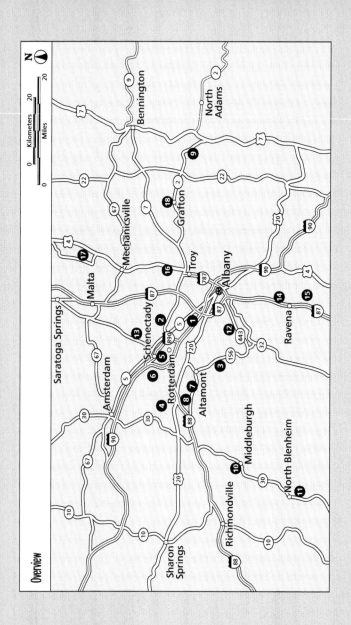

Overview

Acknowledgments

Back in 2010, an author, a photographer, a doctor/guide, and a scientist decided to go hiking together. It sounds like the setup for an esoteric joke, but in reality the four in question were me; my gallant husband, Nic Minetor; our Adirondack 46er friend, Dr. Donna Tuttle; and my lifelong friend Martin Winer. In nine days, we hiked fourteen of the eighteen trails described herein and a couple more that didn't make the "best" cut. To top it off, our good friend and Donna's husband, Dan O'Donnell, kept the chuck wagon humming at home, whipping up a series of energizing meals while we conquered the Albany countryside. As I revisit this book for its second edition, I can't thank these folks enough for their willing and cheerful participation in this escapade and for Donna's generosity with lessons in mountain hiking skills and her watchful eye on our ankles after each of us had turned at least one. I thank Martin for being such a good sport about wandering around in woods after woods, and to Nic, I can only say that I continue to be the luckiest wife in the world.

Many managers of beautiful natural spaces extended their assistance for the first edition. I thank Leslie Reed-Evans of the Williamstown Rural Land Foundation; Colin Campbell of the Taconic Hiking Club; Christopher Hawver of the Albany Pine Bush Preserve Commission; Stephen J. Feeney with Schenectady County; Daniel A. Driscoll of the Mohawk Hudson Land Conservancy; Chris Fallon at John Boyd Thacher State Park; and William Valosin, Joe Craig, and Gina Johnson, National Park Service rangers at Saratoga National Battlefield Park. I'm especially grateful to Harold B.

Vroman for his careful review of my chapter on Vroman's Nose and his kind, handwritten notes.

To the folks at Falcon who have brought so many of my books to careful fruition, I am grateful once again that they make producing a subsequent edition of a hiking book such a streamlined process. And to my agent, Regina Ryan, I extend my thanks for working out so many contractual details early on so another contract is a stress-free experience for me. It's a true gift to spend so much of my career with such a terrific team.

Introduction

Wedged between the Adirondack Mountains to the north and the Allegheny Plateau, arching across its southern boundary, the area around Albany offers some of the most exciting light hiking in Upstate New York, combining outstanding scenery and fascinating geology with the area's healthy respect and appreciation for the value of the outdoors.

The heart of this area's topography lies along the Helderberg Escarpment, a geologic signature that stretches across the county with its highest point well south of the Capital District. From its top—located in John Boyd Thacher State Park and easily viewed from the platforms along the parking lot—viewers enjoy a broad panorama of the southern Adirondack Mountains, the valleys of the Hudson and Mohawk Rivers, and even the Taconic Mountains to the east and the Berkshires beyond. Fossils abound in the escarpment, revealing hundreds of millions of years of natural history, while eons of erosion have left their marks as caves, sinkholes, underground springs, and streams that trickle through cracks and holes in the karst terrain.

With mountains in every direction, wide valleys that still hold farmers' fields and a patchwork of emergent forests, the escarpment, and the confluence of two of New York State's major rivers, it's no wonder that the tri-city area of Albany, Schenectady, and Troy serves up so many hiking treats to its residents and guests.

Venture outside the city proper, and you need not go far to discover the gems that make this area such a find for casual hikers. Northeast of the city and close to Troy, Peebles Island State Park offers an easy, rambling walk around the island's perimeter, with continuous views of the Mohawk River as it flows over a dam and around scattered landforms. Just northwest of the city, the Albany Pine Bush Preserve protects a last remnant of the glacial lake that once covered much of New York State: a set of sandy, sparsely vegetated pine barrens, where ferns and wildflowers vie for footing at the roots of scrub oak and hemlock. To the southwest, Five Rivers Environmental Education Center offers a welcome respite from city life, its woods and open fields brimming with birds, butterflies, and small furry animals.

Extend your adventures beyond Albany County, and your travels will reveal the spectacular views of Schoharie Valley at the end of a vigorous but short hike up the aptly named Vroman's Nose. Cross Schenectady County and explore a series of preserves maintained around kills, the Dutch term for *riverbed* or *water channel*—in this case, a series of merrily splashing creeks that give definition to the otherwise decidedly suburban landscape. Lisha Kill and Plotter Kill Preserves feature fairly rugged hiking up and down central New York's trademark ravines but with an appropriate reward: tumbling water, either in stair-step falls embedded in creeks or cascading from the top of rocky outcroppings. A little farther north, Indian Kill Preserve provides a verdant oasis in the midst of residential development, its trails ambling alongside the creek to a challenging crossing—expect to get your feet wet just about any time of year.

If you like a sprinkle of history mixed into your hiking diet, head northeast of Albany to Saratoga National Historical Park and walk the Wilkinson National Recreation Trail, following in the footsteps of the British regulars as they faced the passion and fury of America's first army. Or head due south of the city to Schodack Island State Park, where explorer Henry Hudson made landfall in the early 1600s and achieved a peaceful first contact with the Mohican Indians.

For some, an "easy" hike is one that doesn't require ropes and technical gear but still offers a good measure of aerobic challenge. If you love to increase your pulse rate and feel the burn in your calves and quads, the Taconic Crest Trail is for you—an out-and-back hike of more than 6 miles with 400 feet of elevation change, topped off by wide-open views of the Taconic Mountains, lots of wild berries in late June and July, and a geologic wonder called the Snow Hole at the end of the "out" leg. (You're welcome to backpack into Vermont by continuing north on this trail, which extends 35.4 miles north.)

Finally, if you hike only one trail in this book, make it the Indian Ladder Trail in John Boyd Thacher State Park, near Voorheesville in Albany County. There's no better place to experience the dramatic Helderberg Escarpment, enjoy panoramic views of the county's countryside, get up close and personal with towering limestone walls, or slip behind waterfalls that originate high above the trail. Just about 0.75-mile long (one way) but packed with geologic delights, this terrific little trail traces the route Schoharie Indians took as they passed through on trade or hunting expeditions many hundreds of years ago.

Whether you enjoy a quiet stroll in a wooded glen, a rugged day hike to waterfalls and sweeping views, an afternoon's meander with binoculars as songbirds arrive in spring, or a brisk trot along a paved path, you'll find your idea of a great day out in the area around Albany—and with luck, you'll discover some splendid natural spaces you've never visited before.

Weather

Few places can match central New York for its gorgeous spring and summer, when flower fragrances scent the air, leaves fairly burst from the trees with intense emerald shades, and the sky turns cobalt to complement the sunlight.

The sun shines six days out of ten from June through August, and while spring temperatures can linger in the 50s and 60s until June, idyllic summer days average in the 70s and 80s, with occasional spikes into the 90s in June or July, and cooler temperatures at night. Heavy rains often arrive in April, although they rarely last more than a day or two at a time. The Capital District has no dry season, so be prepared for rain any time you visit.

To truly appreciate the transformation to Technicolor spring and summer seasons in Upstate New York, however, we must face the Albany area's legendary winters. Winter temperatures average in the mid-20s, with significant dips into the teens in January, February, and March. Check the wind chill before making a winter hike, as the air can feel much colder than the temperature indicates. The annual February thaw can push temperatures into the 50s for a few days, but the cold will return, usually lasting into mid-April. Snow is guaranteed—an average winter sees about 63 inches, although not all at once. The Albany area sees the highest percentage of sunny days in Upstate New York—as much as 67 percent in summer, and nearly 40 percent even in the doldrums of winter.

Fall equals spring in its spectacle, with days in the 50s and 60s, bright blue skies, and foliage panoramas throughout the area's parks and preserves.

Park and Preserve Regulations

You will find the lands listed in this book both accessible and fairly easy to navigate. Only the state parks listed charge seasonal admission fees (though some preserves suggest a donation).

While some of the parks have picnic areas with trash receptacles, most of the parks, forests, and preserves are "carry-in, carry-out" areas. This means that you must take all your trash with you for disposal outside the park. Glass containers are not permitted in any of the parks.

In all cases, dogs and other pets must be leashed—and some preserves do not permit pets. You will see dogs running free in some parks, but park regulations and county leash laws prohibit this. It's also illegal to leave your dog's droppings in the park; you can face fines for not cleaning up after your pet.

If you're a gun owner, you will need to leave your weapon at home when entering a county park, as only law enforcement officers are permitted to carry guns on these lands. Hunting is permitted on properties managed by the New York State Department of Environmental Conservation, so it's good to wear a blaze orange jacket and hat if you're planning to hike these areas during hunting seasons.

Safety and Preparation

There is little to fear when hiking in Upstate New York, whether you're stepping down into the gorge at Christman Sanctuary or traversing the Great Flats Nature Trail. Some basic safety precautions and intelligent preparation will make all your hikes calamity free.

- **Wear proper footwear.** A good, correctly fitted pair of hiking shoes or boots can make all the difference on a daylong hike or even a short walk. Look for socks that wick away moisture, or add sock liners to your footwear system. Consider higher boots that offer ankle support for hikes that lead through rocky terrain or up and down hills.

- **Carry a first aid kit** to deal with blisters, cuts and scrapes, and insect bites and stings. Insects abound in late spring and summer in central New York, especially near wetlands, ponds, lakes, and creeks, so wear insect repellent and carry after-bite ointment or cream to apply to itchy spots. Poison ivy lines many of these trails, so watch for "leaves of three" and carry a product designed to remove urushiol (the oil in poison ivy) from your skin. Ask your pharmacist for recommendations.

- **Carry water.** Don't try drinking from the rivers, creeks, ponds, or other bodies of water unless you can filter or treat the water first. Every waterway in the country may carry pathogens like giardia, cryptosporidium, shigella, or a range of others that can result in serious gastrointestinal illness. Your best bet is to carry your own—at least a quart for any hike and up to a gallon in hot weather.

- **Dress in layers**, no matter the season. If you're a vigorous hiker, you'll want to peel off a layer or two even in the dead of winter. On a summer evening, the air can cool suddenly after sunset, and rain clouds can erupt with little preamble.

- **Bring your mobile phone.** All but the most remote trails in central New York have mobile coverage, so if you do get into a jam, help is a phone call away. (Set it to vibrate while you're on trail, however, as a courtesy to the rest of us.)

- **Leave wildlife alone.** Central New York State once was home to the timber rattlesnake, but scientists believe this species to be extirpated from most of the areas covered in this book—though they may be possible along the Taconic Crest. Black bear sightings do happen occasionally, especially in mountain pass areas like the Taconic Crest and in state parks that border the Adirondacks and Catskills. As a general rule, don't approach wildlife of any kind. If you do see a bear, don't go closer to it; if your presence changes its behavior, you're too close. Keep your distance, and the bear will most likely do the same. Some cases of rabies in raccoons have been reported in the area; generally, it's best to steer clear of these animals when they're seen in daylight.

- **Check for ticks.** Deer ticks have multiplied exponentially throughout New York State, and they carry Lyme disease, which can be debilitating. If a tick bites you and embeds itself in your skin, don't panic—the Albany County Department of Health notes that it takes 24 to 36 hours for the tick to transfer Lyme disease to you. Remove the tick with tweezers (don't touch it with your hands), and watch for three to thirty days to see if a target-shaped rash develops. If you develop symptoms like fatigue, weakness, fever, headache, and/or joint or muscle pain, schedule a Lyme disease test through your primary care physician. You'll find the latest information about Lyme disease prevention and testing at https://www.health.ny.gov/diseases/communicable/lyme/.

Zero Impact

Many trails in the Albany area are heavily used year round. As trail users and advocates, we must be especially vigilant to make sure our passage leaves no lasting mark. Here are some basic guidelines for preserving trails in the region:

- Pack out all your own trash, including biodegradable items like orange peels. You might also pack out garbage left by less considerate hikers.

- Don't approach or feed any wild creatures—the gray squirrel eyeing your snack food is best able to survive if it remains self-reliant. Feeding ducks and geese can spread illnesses between the birds when they come into contact while chasing bits of bread or corn. Please don't feed them.

- Don't pick wildflowers or gather rocks, antlers, feathers, and other treasures along the trail. Removing these items will only take away from the next hiker's experience.

- Avoid damaging trailside soils and plants by remaining on the established route. This is also a good rule of thumb for avoiding poison ivy and poison sumac, common regional trailside irritants.

- Be courteous by not making loud noises while hiking.

- Many of these trails are multiuse, which means you'll share them with other hikers, trail runners, bikers, and equestrians. Familiarize yourself with the proper trail etiquette, yielding the trail when appropriate.

- Use restrooms or outhouses at trailheads or along the trail.

Land Management Agencies

These government and nonprofit organizations manage most of the public lands described in this guide. They can provide further information on these hikes and other trails in the greater Syracuse area.

- Mohawk Hudson Land Conservancy, PO Box 567, Slingerlands 12159; (518) 436-6346; www.mohawk hudson.org
- New York State Canal Corporation, 200 Southern Blvd., Albany 12201; (800) 4CANAL4 (422-6254); https://www.canals.ny.gov
- New York State Department of Environmental Conservation, Region 4, 1130 North Westcott Rd., Schenectady 12306; (518) 357-2234; www.dec.ny.gov
- New York State Office of Parks, Recreation and Historic Preservation, Empire State Plaza, Agency Building 1, Albany 12238; (518) 474-0456; https://parks.ny.gov
- Schenectady County Economic Development and Planning, 107 Nott Ter., Schaffer Heights Ste. 303, Schenectady 12308; (518) 386-2225; https://schenectady countyny.gov/ed-planning
- The Nature Conservancy, 195 New Karner Rd., Albany 12205; (518) 690-7850; www.nature.org/en-us/about-us/where-we-work/united-states/new-york/

How to Use This Guide

This guide is designed to be simple and easy to use. Each hike is described, with a map and summary information that delivers the trail's vital statistics, including length, difficulty, fees and permits, park hours, canine compatibility, and trail contacts. Directions to the trailhead are also provided, along with a general description of what you'll see along the way. A detailed route finder (Miles and Directions) sets forth mileages between significant landmarks along the trail.

Hike Selection

This guide describes trails that are accessible to every hiker, whether visiting from out of town or living in the greater Albany area. The hikes are no longer than 8 miles round trip, and some are considerably shorter. They range in difficulty from flat excursions perfect for a family outing to more challenging treks along the area's gorges, into ravines, and on rocky terrain. While these trails are among the best, keep in mind that nearby trails, often in the same park or preserve, may offer options better suited to your needs. I've spaced hikes throughout the Albany, Rensselaer, Schenectady, Schoharie, and Saratoga County areas, so regardless of the starting point, you'll find a great easy day hike nearby.

Difficulty Ratings

These are all easy hikes, but *easy* is a relative term. Some would argue that no hike involving any kind of upward elevation change is easy, but in the Albany area, on the edges of the Adirondack, Taconic, and Catskill Mountain Ranges, hills and ravines are a fact of life. To aid in the selection of a hike that suits particular needs and abilities, each is rated easy, moderate, or more challenging. Bear in mind that even most challenging routes can be made easy by hiking within your limits and taking rests when you need them.

- **Easy** hikes are generally short and flat, taking no longer than an hour to complete.
- **Moderate** hikes involve increased distance and relatively mild changes in elevation and will take 1 to 2 hours to complete.
- **More challenging** hikes feature some steep stretches, greater distances, and generally take longer than 2 hours to complete.

These are completely subjective ratings—consider that what you think is easy is entirely dependent on your level of fitness and the adequacy of your gear (primarily shoes). If you are hiking with a group, you should select a hike with a rating that's appropriate for the least fit and prepared in your party.

Approximate hiking times are based on the assumption that, on flat ground, most walkers average 2 miles per hour. Adjust that rate by the steepness of the terrain and your level of fitness (subtract time if you're an aerobic animal and add time if you're hiking with kids), and you have a ballpark hiking duration. Be sure to add more time if you plan to picnic or take part in other activities, like bird watching or photography.

Trail Finder

Best Hikes for Birders

5 Great Flats Nature Trail
7 Wolf Creek Falls Preserve
12 Five Rivers Environmental Education Center: North
    Loop Trail
17 Saratoga National Historical Park: Wilkinson National
    Recreation Trail

Best Hikes for Waterfalls

2 Lisha Kill Preserve
3 John Boyd Thacher State Park: Indian Ladder Trail
6 Plotter Kill Preserve
7 Wolf Creek Falls Preserve
8 Christman Sanctuary
13 Indian Kill Nature Preserve

Best Hikes for Water Views

5 Great Flats Nature Trail
8 Christman Sanctuary
15 Lewis A. Swyer Preserve
16 Peebles Island State Park
18 Grafton Lakes State Park: Long Pond Trail

Best Hikes for Fall Foliage

1 Albany Pine Bush Preserve: Karner Barrens East
4 Schenectady County Forest Preserve
14 Schodack Island State Park
17 Saratoga National Historical Park: Wilkinson National Recreation Trail
18 Grafton Lakes State Park: Long Pond Trail

Best Hikes for Panoramic Views

3 John Boyd Thacher State Park: Indian Ladder Trail
9 Taconic Crest Trail to the Snow Hole
10 Vroman's Nose
11 Mine Kill State Park
16 Peebles Island State Park

Map Legend

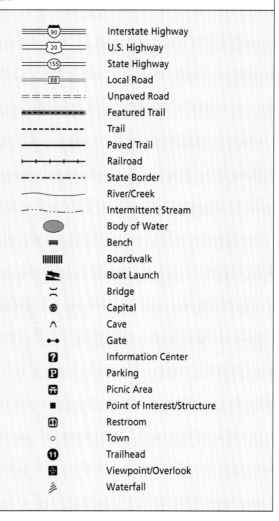

90	Interstate Highway
20	U.S. Highway
155	State Highway
88	Local Road
	Unpaved Road
	Featured Trail
	Trail
	Paved Trail
	Railroad
	State Border
	River/Creek
	Intermittent Stream
	Body of Water
	Bench
	Boardwalk
	Boat Launch
	Bridge
	Capital
	Cave
	Gate
	Information Center
	Parking
	Picnic Area
	Point of Interest/Structure
	Restroom
	Town
	Trailhead
	Viewpoint/Overlook
	Waterfall

1 Albany Pine Bush Preserve

Karner Barrens East

Immerse yourself in the Albany County that existed centuries ago as you traverse emerging pine barrens rising from scrub oak woodlands.

Distance: 2.2-mile loop
Approximate hiking time: 1.25 hours
Difficulty: Easy
Trail surface: Packed sand, then dirt path through woods
Best seasons: Apr through Nov
Other trail users: Cross-country skiers, trail runners, horseback riders, mountain bikers
Canine compatibility: Dogs permitted on leash
Fees and permits: None
Schedule: Open daily, dawn to dusk
Maps: Available at the Discovery Center at the preserve entrance during open hours; also at

https://albanypinebush.org/corecode/uploads/document6/uploaded_pdfs/corecode/1-KarnerBarrens_14.pdf
Trailhead facilities: Restrooms at Discovery Center
Trail contact: Albany Pine Bush Preserve Commission, 195 New Karner Rd. #1, Albany; (518) 456-0655; www.albanypinebush.org
Special considerations: Wear long pants to guard against deer ticks. Hunting is permitted in season; check the website or at the Discovery Center for seasons and restrictions.

Finding the trailhead: From Albany take the New York State Thruway (I-90) east or west to I-87 (Northway) North. Continue to exit 2W (Route 5 West). Drive west about 2 miles and turn left (south) at the light onto NY 155 South (New Karner Road). Continue 1 mile to the second light, and turn left (east) to the Discovery Center. The trail begins behind the center. **GPS:** N42 43.093' / W73 51.854'.

The Hike

It's not often that we have an opportunity to see pine barrens, especially those in inland locations away from ocean coasts. The Albany Pine Bush Preserve offers a particularly high-quality chance to explore an area that had lost its original character to development and invasive species but is now reemerging—the result of a careful program of prescribed burning and mowing down of the scrub oak that crowded out the original pitch pine and its counterparts.

What is all this sand doing in the middle of Upstate New York? The sand is the last remnant of a vast glacial lake that formed as the ice melted at the end of the last Ice Age, 15,000 years ago. As the glaciers melted and the lake formed, a network of rivers flowed into the lake and brought silt and fine sand with their currents, depositing these materials into the water. The lake disappeared over the ensuing thousands of years, leaving sand dunes that eventually became home to prairie grasses, densely packed shrubs, pitch pine, and occasional ponds—all held together by the vegetation that adapted to this sandy soil. Today, these species depend on the sand to survive.

Your hike follows the perimeter of Karner Barrens East, an easily accessed series of trails that begins at the Discovery Center. The barrens here are some of the strongest and most vibrant in the preserve, bringing you deep into fields of scrub oak and many other shrubs and then leading into a pitch pine forest shared by oak, hickory, and maple trees.

The unusual ecosystem provides a home for lush beds of ferns that blanket the forest floor, their intense, lacy greenery one of the highlights of this hike. Watch for all kinds of wildflowers edging the path, from the wild blue lupines on the blue trail to marsh marigolds, columbine, and bunchberry. Field sparrows' bouncing ping-pong-ball song rises from the open meadows, and wood thrushes call from deep in the woods. Keep an eye out for chipmunks in twos and threes dashing across the path, and look for evidence of white-tailed deer munching on leaves on the low tree branches.

Miles and Directions

0.0   Park at the Discovery Center and begin at the trailhead behind the building. You'll see a wooden information kiosk at the trailhead. Start by following the yellow trail to the right (yellow plastic disks with white printing serve as trail markers). The first part of the trail parallels New Karner Road.

0.4   A connector trail goes right. Continue straight on the yellow trail. In about 100 feet, the blue trail goes left and the yellow trail goes straight (southeast); go straight on the yellow trail.

0.7   An unmarked trail goes right. Continue straight (east) on the yellow trail.

0.8   A white connector trail goes back and to the left. Continue straight, passing through an area with high shrubs, many of which are scrub oak. Some pine trees have broken through the dense shrub cover.

1.0   A split-rail fence blocks a closed trail. Bear left on the yellow trail.

1.2   A white connector trail goes left. Continue straight (northeast) on the yellow trail. The woodland around you is home to an assortment of pitch pine, oak, hickory, and maple. In some areas, the pines have become dominant.

1.4   Cross an unmarked trail deep in the woods and continue straight on the yellow trail. Begin a downhill slope in hilly terrain. You may notice a concentration of tent caterpillar nests in the angles of trees throughout this area. As you descend

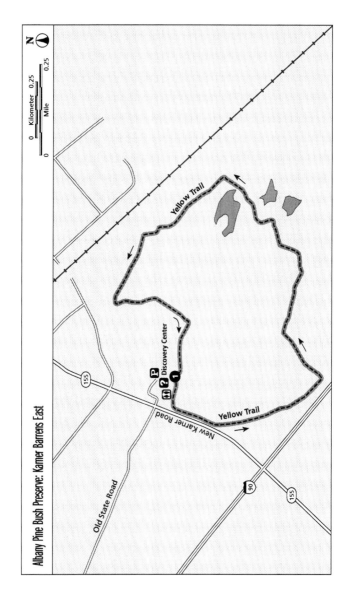

Albany Pine Bush Preserve: Karner Barrens East

the hill, don't miss the closely packed ferns thriving on the forest floor.

1.9 A split-rail fence blocks another closed trail to the right. Continue straight ahead (south) on the yellow trail. Listen for eastern towhees, great-crested flycatchers, and yellow warblers as you pass through these woods. Soon you come to an area of thick shrubbery with far fewer tall trees.

2.0 A white connector trail goes left. Continue straight on the yellow trail.

2.2 The yellow trail turns right. In about 100 feet, pass a trail to the right with green markers and a bridge over a stream—this is the short Discovery Trail. Take this to the Discovery Center.

2 Lisha Kill Preserve

A merry stream, a forested ravine, and a fragrant wood of hemlock and white pine make this hidden preserve a Niskayuna neighborhood favorite.

Distance: 2-mile loop
Approximate hiking time: 1 hour
Difficulty: Easy
Trail surface: Well-packed dirt path through woods
Best seasons: Apr through Nov
Other trail users: Cross-country skiers, trail runners
Canine compatibility: Dogs permitted on leash
Fees and permits: None
Schedule: Open daily, dawn to dusk
Maps: The Nature Conservancy: www.nature.org/content/dam/tnc/nature/en/documents/lisha-kill-map-2015.pdf
Trailhead facilities: None. Do not drink from the stream.
Trail contact: The Nature Conservancy, 195 New Karner Rd., Albany 12205; (518) 690-7850; www.nature.org/en-us/get-involved/how-to-help/places-we-protect/lisha-kill-natural-area/
Special considerations: What goes down must come up: Be prepared for a couple significant uphill sections.

Finding the trailhead: From Albany take I-87 (Northway) to exit 6. From here, take NY 7 west for 4.4 miles. Turn right on Mohawk Road, and continue for 0.7 mile to Rosendale Road. Drive 1.1 miles to the parking area on your left (south), about 0.3 mile past River Road. Look for the white Lisha Kill Preserve sign. Park in the lot behind the closed white building. **GPS:** N42 47.770' / W73 51.588'.

The Hike

This lovely little preserve—just 108 acres, 40 of which are old-growth forest of eastern hemlock and eastern white pine—nearly met a miserable end in 1963, when state government officials proposed bulldozing it to make way for NY 7. Land preservation was a new idea in the early 1960s, but a group of concerned neighbors realized the need for action and contacted the Nature Conservancy to gain the organization's support for their cause. Today we can enjoy the products of their success.

The hike follows the main trail through the preserve, quickly descending to Lisha Kill Stream and wandering the bottom of a well-forested ravine, then climbing back out (a difference of about 200 feet) to follow the ravine edge through old-growth woods. In addition to the hemlock and pine, you're likely to find yourself in the midst of a variety of invasive shrubs that have taken hold here. The fact that Japanese barberry, bush honeysuckle, and multiflora rose do not belong in this wild place makes them no less beautiful, and the floral scents mingle with the evergreens to deliver natural, rejuvenating aromatherapy.

In addition to the remarkable forest, keep an eye out for barred and great-horned owls that nest and breed in this preserve. It's not uncommon to spot either of these impressive birds in daylight, and their calls are unmistakable after dark or in the wee hours before dawn.

Miles and Directions

0.0   From the parking area, follow the red trail—designated by plastic markers that sport red arrows on a green background.

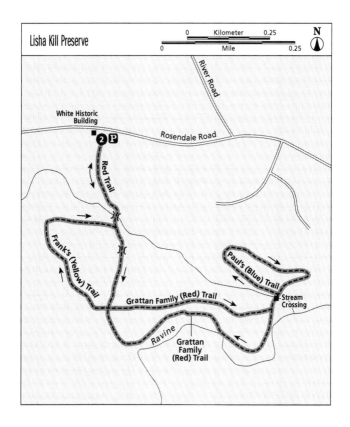

Right away, you'll begin a gentle descent to Lisha Kill Stream.

0.2 Cross a small bridge over the stream and continue on the red trail.

0.3 At the junction with the yellow trail (yellow arrows on blue markers), continue straight (south) on the red trail. Cross another small bridge over a wet area.

0.4 At this three-way intersection, a sign indicates that the yellow trail is Frank's Trail. This trail goes right. The red trail goes straight and to the left (east). Go left on the red trail.

0.6 A blue trail goes left here. We learn from a sign that the blue trail is called Paul's Trail. Turn left (northwest) on Paul's Trail; the red trail continues to the right. You're following the solid blue markers now.

0.7 Cross the creek on smooth, flat rocks. (This may be tougher in spring, when snowmelt swells the creek.) At the T intersection, turn left—don't cross the tiny stream that flows here.

0.9 Markers for a white trail appear; the white trail goes off left. Skip this and continue straight on the blue trail. When you reach an intersection with the red trail, turn left and descend to the creek. Turn right and walk along the creek at the bottom of the ravine.

1.0 A fairly steep climb out of the ravine follows, and then the red trail traces the edge of the crevasse at its top. Note the beautiful views of the treetops that grow taller than the ravine.

1.6 As you approach the edge of the ravine on the red trail, there's a Danger sign. The trail does not actually come close to the ravine edge, but the sign reminds you not to leave the trail. You are entirely safe as long as you stay on the trail. Reach an intersection with the yellow trail, and turn left (northwest) on this yellow trail.

1.8 When you reconnect with the red trail, turn left (north) and begin the final climb out of the ravine. This is the downhill slope you enjoyed at the beginning of your hike.

2.0 You're back at the top of the ravine and at the end of your hike. Complete the last few feet to the parking area.

3 John Boyd Thacher State Park

Indian Ladder Trail

Limestone cliffs, spectacular valley views, hanging gardens, jagged rock formations, and coves behind waterfalls: This is the must-see trail in the Capital Region.

Distance: 1.6-mile loop

Approximate hiking time: 1 hour

Difficulty: Easy

Trail surface: Dirt path, some stairs

Best seasons: May through Oct

Other trail users: Hikers only

Canine compatibility: Dogs permitted on leash

Fees and permits: A fee is charged per vehicle on weekends and holidays only; free all other days

Schedule: Open year round, sunrise to sunset

Maps: https://store.avenza.com/products/john-boyd-thacher-state-park-trail-map-south-new-york-state-parks-map

Trailhead facilities: Restrooms and water fountains are at each end of the trail. A concession stand at the Overlook is open on weekends.

Trail contact: Thacher State Park, 830 Thacher Park Rd., Voorheesville 12186; (518) 872-1237; https://parks.ny.gov/parks/thacher/details.aspx

Special considerations: Some steep drop-offs and views from high places; not recommended for very young children. This hike features 110 stairs going down at its outset and 110 going up at the end of the gorge hike.

Finding the trailhead: From Voorheesville, take NY 85A (Helderberg Parkway/New Salem Road) west and south to the junction with NY 85 (New Scotland Road). Turn right (west, then south) on NY 85 and continue to the junction with NY 157. Turn right (west) on NY 157 and continue to the park. **GPS:** N42 39.106' / W74 00.426'.

The Hike

Of the many excellent hiking opportunities in the greater Albany area, Indian Ladder Trail stands out as the best representation of central New York's geological story: The hike traces an edge of the Helderberg Escarpment, where the collision of continents hundreds of millions of years ago forced limestone, sandstone, and shale peaks up from the depths of the Earth's bedrock. Over eons, wind and weather wore away the sharp peaks and left behind this long range of cliffs, breaking away great limestone slabs and leaving a rock wall perpendicular to the valley floor at its base.

Fast-forward to about 1,000 years ago, when the Schoharie Indians came through here regularly on a path along the rock ridgeline we see today. Descending from the cliff above on makeshift ladders, the Indians followed the path behind waterfalls and over tricky rock faces, then climbed a ladder at the other end and returned to higher ground. Today, we call this the Indian Ladder Trail, but the ladders are gone—although they were in use as recently as the 1950s—and hikers now climb down sturdy metal staircases to gain access to the visual riches below.

Towering limestone walls, waterfalls originating above and below the trail, and overhangs that allow you to stand behind tumbling waters are just a few of the delights this trail presents. Remember to look behind you to catch the hanging gardens that spring forth when water seeps through porous rock walls and to peer deep into holes in the rock to glimpse the origins of trickling streams. Don't be surprised if a chipmunk comes up to your shoe and waits expectantly—wildlife here seem to know that people mean food, but feeding the chipmunks or any other animals is illegal. Try not to be taken in by a striped, 4-inch-high bandit.

You can walk the Indian Ladder Trail to its end, turn around and walk back on the same trail, or climb the 110 steps at the far end and return on the level trail at the rim of the cliff. The rim trail delivers the panoramic valley views and provides an easy return route if you've had enough of stairs, rocks, and ledges.

Miles and Directions

0.0   Park in the last lot at the end of the bank of parking areas. Before you begin your hike, stop to enjoy the view of the valley below. To your right (east), you can see the very tall building standing parallel to four identical smaller buildings: These are all part of Empire State Plaza, the center of the Capital District in downtown Albany. The trail begins at the stone staircase to your left (northwest). Follow the aqua blazes.

0.2   Emerge from the trail along the rim in a mowed picnic area. Continue along the edge on the trail, which gives you another chance to admire the view.

0.4   At the end of the picnic area, take the stairs down. There are 110 steps in all, some metal and some stone. You'll come to a part of the staircase with a low ceiling—a natural overhang that's about 4.5 feet high. Stoop to go through it, and come out on the Talus Slope, a particularly striking area of rock formations. Go down another eleven steps into an area where water drips down the rock wall, creating hanging gardens of ferns and mosses.

0.5   You're behind Mine Lot Falls, under an overhang that extends the falls out in front of you. Note that there's water coming down behind you as well, pouring over the rock wall. The water wore holes in the rock over many years. It's easy to spot the wet areas because plant life grows here wherever

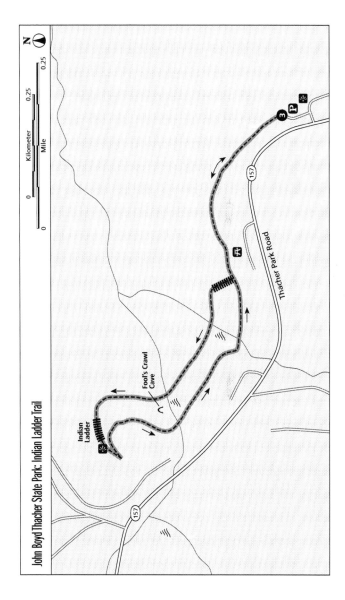

John Boyd Thacher State Park: Indian Ladder Trail

there's running water. From here, cross a short boardwalk and go down eleven steps toward the second falls.

0.6 The second waterfall is actually two falls, one cascading from above and one falling just in front of you. Watch your step, as the stream that feeds this waterfall crosses the stone path here.

0.7 In this alcove, you'll find Fool's Crawl Cave, on the course of an underground stream. Look down the rocks to see the stream tumble down the cliff face.

0.8 This huge natural archway is worth exploration—there are openings for shallow caves at either side. Continue to the staircase at the end of the path. It's sixty-two stairs up to a scenic landing and twelve steps down from the landing to a viewing platform.

0.9 The viewing deck offers a fairly unobstructed view of the valley below—a strikingly green sight in spring and summer. When you're ready, return up the twelve steps and go up forty-eight more to the cliff rim. Turn left (southeast) and walk back along the rim trail (still blazed aqua) to the picnic area.

1.1 Cross the stream on stepped rocks straight ahead, or go around to your right about 100 feet to take the bridge across.

1.2 Join the paved path and continue on the bridge over the stream. The second waterfall you saw below originates here.

1.3 Steps lead down to the path you followed on your way in, along the rim of the cliff. Take this path back to the parking area.

1.6 Arrive back at the parking area.

4 Schenectady County Forest Preserve

Tucked into the hills, this north–country forest and open wetland features remnants of the farming community that thrived here more than a century ago.

Distance: 1.5-mile loop
Approximate hiking time: 1 hour
Difficulty: Easy
Trail surface: Dirt path, some boardwalk
Best seasons: May through Oct
Other trail users: Cross-country skiers, hunters in season
Canine compatibility: Dogs permitted on leash
Fees and permits: None
Schedule: Open dawn to dusk
Maps: www.alltrails.com/trail/us/new-york/schenectady-county-blue-trail

Trailhead facilities: None
Trail contact: Schenectady County Economic Development and Planning Department, 107 Nott Ter., Schaffer Heights Ste. 303, Schenectady 12308; (518) 386-2225; https://schenectady countyny.gov/ed-planning
Special considerations: The trail can be very muddy in wet seasons. Hunting is permitted Nov 15 through Dec 15, so wear blaze orange if you hike at that time.

Finding the trailhead: From I-90 (New York State Thruway), take exit 25 in Schenectady and follow I-890 west to Campbell Road (exit 2A). Turn right (west) on Putnam Road, and go 1.7 miles to NY 159 (Mariaville Road). Turn right (north) on NY 159 and continue about 4.5 miles to the intersection of NY 159 and Lake Road. Turn left (west) on Lake Road and drive 4 miles to the county forest preserve entrance. **GPS:** N42 48.098' / W74 09.271'.

The Hike

A favorite among Duanesburg residents, Schenectady County Forest Preserve provides a delightful mix of habitats in just 102 acres. Here a natural wetland; a forest of native hardwoods, including maple, oak, and beech; and a plantation of red pine trees surround a man-made pond created as recently as 1982, providing a home to such critters as eastern chipmunks, gray squirrels, common garter snakes, and spring peepers, those tiny frogs that are such fun to find along the trail.

The preserve delivers a slice of history, as well, with the remains of James Duane's homestead foundation still visible—if you look for them—among the thriving wildflowers and ferns west of the trail's first 0.1 mile. Multiflora roses and the oversized leaves of rhubarb remind visitors that this was once a populated property, and the ruins of stone walls that once divided the fields now serve as hiking landmarks.

Look for jack-in-the-pulpit, marsh marigolds, many fern species, and red trillium as you wander the woods on the easy loop trail. A boundary of flowering shrubs lines the path, giving way to the red pine plantation—a grove of trees planted in 1933 and 1934, now grown into a mature forest that covers the trail with its soft needles.

As you round the last bend in the loop, don't miss the old cemetery down a short trail to your left. Most of the headstones are no longer readable, but the marker for Daniel Wiggins, who bought some of the land from Cornelius Duane in the 1800s, still tells us that he was laid to rest here in 1828. If you love local history, be sure to read the plaques that detail some of the landowners' chronology, spanning more than 200 years of ownership, agriculture, and development.

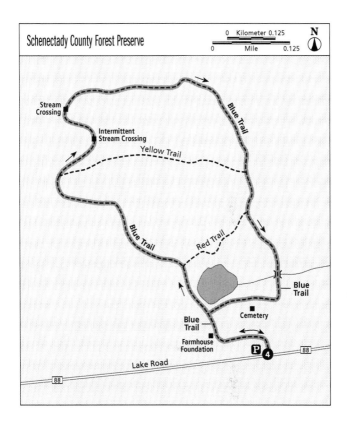

Schenectady County Forest Preserve

Stream Crossing

Intermittent Stream Crossing

Yellow Trail

Blue Trail

Blue Trail

Red Trail

Blue Trail

Cemetery

Blue Trail

Farmhouse Foundation

Lake Road

Miles and Directions

0.0 Park in the lot off Lake Road. The trail is on the left (west) end of the parking area. Turn right (north) at the first intersection.

0.1 Pass through the former Duane homestead. If you'd like to search for the farmhouse foundation, you can find it in the overgrown wildflowers and plants to your left (west).

0.2 Turn left at the next intersection, and note the wild roses and rhubarb growing to your right. A path to the pond appears on your right (east). Continue straight.

0.5 The yellow trail goes right. This straight trail bisects the loop; if you like, you can cut across to shorten your hike. Otherwise, continue straight (north) as you begin the blue trail. Enjoy the view of the wetland area from this trail segment.

0.6 Reach a small stream. Cross with care; it can be muddy in this area after a rain.

0.7 A board over a stream allows you to cross here. From this point, the trail continues into slightly higher (and much drier) ground as you enter the red pine plantation. The deciduous trees in the next stretch of trail include old-growth maples—look for the tree with the double trunk.

1.1 The red trail goes straight into a loop around the pond. Bear left (south) instead, and look for arrows painted on the trees to guide you here. This is a very swampy area, but two-plank boardwalks over some of the wettest spots aid your progress.

1.3 A nice bridge provides a wide view of the open area around the wetland and the pond. The trail turns right and goes up a short but pronounced incline into a woodland filled with northern hardwoods. The trail to the cemetery appears on your left (it's marked). Take the short detour if you like, and return to the main trail when you're ready to proceed. Turn left (southeast) to return to the parking area.

1.5 Arrive back at the parking lot.

5 Great Flats Nature Trail

Where woods meet wetland, habitats abound—so bring your binoculars and watch closely for birds, amphibians, and little animals as you circle this remarkable preserve.

Distance: 2-mile loop
Approximate hiking time: 1 hour
Difficulty: Easy
Trail surface: Dirt path, some boardwalk
Best seasons: May through Oct
Other trail users: Birders, cross-country skiers
Canine compatibility: Dogs permitted on leash
Fees and permits: None
Schedule: Open dawn to dusk

Maps: *National Geographic Topo!* New York/New Jersey edition
Trailhead facilities: None
Trail contact: Schenectady County Economic Development and Planning Department, 107 Nott Ter., Schaffer Heights Ste. 303, Schenectady 12308; (518) 386-2225; https://schenectady countyny.gov/ed-planning
Special considerations: The trail can be very muddy in wet seasons. Insect repellent is a must!

Finding the trailhead: From I-890 in Schenectady, take exit 2A to West Campbell Road. The parking area is just off West Campbell Road at the junction with exit 2A. **GPS:** N42 48.834' / W73 58.945'.

The Hike

Shoulder-high vegetation along a narrow path through wetlands; thickly forested woodlands giving way to sunny glades filled with local ferns; foliage-rich marshes that provide homes to swamp sparrows, marsh wrens, and dabbling ducks—these are the treasures you'll find at Great

Flats, a carefully protected preserve on the border between the city of Schenectady and the town of Rotterdam. You'd be hard-pressed to find a more unlikely place for a nature park—right across from a major mall in a congested city setting—but it goes to Schenectady County's credit that this important swath of natural land continues to exist, despite pressure to use the land for construction of a mall back in the 1960s.

Originally the property of the area's indigenous Iroquois people, Great Flats found its way into the Dutch settlers' consciousness all the way back in 1661, when a group of these settlers requested permission from then-governor Peter Stuyvesant to buy this land from the Iroquois. The native people had cleared the land and used it to farm crops, so the Dutch citizens saw the value of the excellent drainage here along the Mohawk River. They bought the land for an unspecified sum and began farming it. Two centuries later, the Great Flats Aquifer became a significant water source for the city of Schenectady and the town of Rotterdam, and today it continues to supply more than 54 million gallons of water daily to the surrounding communities.

The hike passes through a stretch of woodland filled with leafy trees and flowering shrubs in the understory to the wetland. Here a boardwalk leads into the dense reeds, nodding fronds of phragmites, and bursting cattails, quickly descending to ground level and becoming a packed-earth trail through the wetland. The path reenters the woods and winds through a drier area before returning to the wetland, leading you to a blind from which it's easy to observe long-legged wading birds, ducks, and geese, especially in the early morning and at sunset.

Miles and Directions

0.0   Park in the lot off West Campbell Road. Take the mowed-grass path into the woods.

0.2   At the T intersection, turn right (northwest). (The path to the left goes out to West Campbell Road.)

0.4   At the next T intersection, turn right (north). There are lots of flowering shrubs and trees here.

0.5   You've reached the first boardwalk. Turn right (northeast) and take the boardwalk to its end. Continue straight on the dirt path that leads off the boardwalk. A pretty pond comes into view on the right (east).

0.6   Traverse another section of boardwalk. Shortly after this, the trail ascends very slightly but enough to change the character of the land from wetland to woods.

0.8   A tiny stream passes under the trail. Skunk cabbage has been known to grow to the right of this stretch; see if you can detect its scent. When you reach a T in the trail, go left (south). Watch for wild raspberries growing close to the ground.

0.9   Reach another stretch of boardwalk. A tree came down here with great force, smashing through the platform—you may need to work your way around it on the ground.

1.0   Another stretch of boardwalk helps you through this wet area. To your right there's a blind for viewing wildlife without detection. Check for wading and swimming birds, like the great blue and green heron, American bittern, Virginia rail, sora, mallards, Canada geese, and other water-loving bird species.

1.1   The boardwalk ends at a trail junction. The right-turning trail goes into the woods, while the straight trail continues through the wetland. Go straight (northeast).

1.2   Turn right (southeast) at the next intersection. Then turn left and proceed to the end of the spur trail, which takes you to a nice view of the pond. When you're ready, turn around

Great Flats Nature Trail

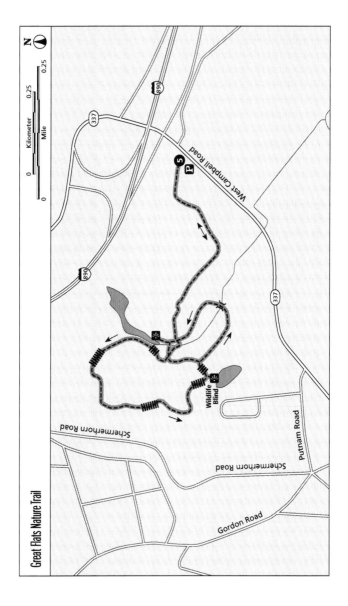

and return to the main trail. You can proceed to the exit from here, but instead take the trail to the right (south), through the woods, for an additional loop.

1.4 A boardwalk bridge crosses calm water.

1.5 You've completed the woodland loop. Turn right (east) and stay on the main trail. Turn right again at the next intersection (you've been here before), and stay on the main trail until you reach the parking area.

2.0 Arrive back at the parking area.

6 Plotter Kill Preserve

A rugged gorge, two waterfalls, and the confluence of a river and a creek provide plenty of natural scenery to admire and explore.

Distance: 2.2-mile figure eight
Approximate hiking time: 1.5 hours
Difficulty: Moderate
Trail surface: Dirt path, some boardwalk
Best seasons: Apr through Oct
Other trail users: Snowshoe hikers in winter
Canine compatibility: Dogs permitted on leash
Fees and permits: None
Schedule: Open dawn to dusk

Maps: www.alltrails.com/parks/us/new-york/plotter-kill-nature-preserve
Trailhead facilities: None
Trail contact: Schenectady County Economic Development and Planning Department, 107 Nott Ter., Schaffer Heights Ste. 303, Schenectady 12308; (518) 386-2225; https://schenectadycountyny.gov/ed-planning
Special considerations: Waterfalls are at their best in early spring and frozen in winter.

Finding the trailhead: The preserve's street address is 3953 Mariaville Road in Schenectady. Take the New York State Thruway (I-90) to exit 25 in Schenectady, and follow I-890 west to Campbell Road (exit 2A). From Campbell Road, turn right (west) on Putnam Road. Continue 1.7 miles to NY 159 (Mariaville Road). Turn right (north) on NY 159 and continue 1.9 miles to the Plotter Kill Preserve parking lot on the right (north). **GPS:** N42 49.538' / W74 03.100'.

The Hike

Some bodies of water came into being when glaciers scooped great bowls into the earth and filled them with ice melt. Others were fingers of glacial sculpture, crevasses that became rivers at the end of the Ice Age. In the case of Plotter Kill, melting ice came at the landscape in a great torrent of rushing water, the sheer force of which sliced a gorge and filled the kill, or creek, that we see here today.

The result is a marvelous hike to two waterfalls—one 60 feet high, the other somewhat smaller—through lush, rolling terrain positively loaded with wildflowers, ferns, fascinating fungi, and tall trees.

With all this being said, it's fair to warn you that Plotter Kill can pose some hiking challenges, even on its easiest trails. Good views of the waterfalls come at the end of downhill stretches that require an uphill climb back to the top of the gorge, while views from the top often appear at the end of long inclines. In spring, water runs down some of these trails into the kill, creating muddy slip-slides down the middle of the trail.

This hike follows one of the easiest routes in the 632-acre preserve, which will bring you to both the Upper and Lower Falls from several viewpoints at the top and bottom of the gorge. In addition to Plotter Kill, you'll follow the preserve boundary until you reach adjacent Rynex Creek, then come back along the creek to one of the preserve's best waterfall vantage points.

Miles and Directions

0.0 From the parking area on NY 159, take the trail to the right of the sign with the map. You will see red and blue blazes or flags (ribbons) here. Follow the red trail to start.

0.1 At the intersection with the blue trail, continue straight (northeast) on the red trail.

0.2 Cross a bridge over a wet area.

0.4 At the intersection, turn left (northwest) and follow the blue blazes. The path to the right leads to private property. Turn right (northeast) at the T intersection on the edge of the gorge, and continue to the Lower Falls Overlook. This is a high vantage point above the falls. When you're ready, go back to the T intersection and continue to your right (southwest) on the blue trail.

0.6 Cross a small stream on rocks. At the T intersection, turn left (southwest) and follow the blue blazes.

0.7 Follow the narrow path to the right to the Upper Falls Overlook (you'll see a fence). When you're ready, continue on the blue trail to the next intersection, and go straight (southwest).

0.8 Turn right (north) on the wooden steps. [If you'd like to shorten your walk, turn left (south) to go back to the parking area.] Cross the bridge over Plotter Kill, and then turn left (west). Follow the red blazes until you reach the yellow trail, and turn left on yellow. Shortly, yellow turns right—follow it and start a walk up a potentially muddy streambed. When you come to an intersection marked with an arrow for the Old Gifford Homestead Trail, turn right on the Highland Trail. Begin a long incline to the top.

1.2 Reach the top of the incline. From here the trail continues along a level path through drier woods of leafy and evergreen trees.

1.5 At the intersection the yellow trail goes right and left. The left (north) path is a spur trail to Rynex Creek. Bear right (east), and cross a little bridge over a stream.

1.8 At this critical intersection, the red trail goes left (northeast) and onto a much longer route through the rest of the park. To your right (southwest) the trail leads back to the preserve entrance. The trail downhill in front of you leads to a terrific river-level view of the Lower Falls. You can choose to skip this view and continue on the path to the parking area, or you can walk down the 200-foot trail to the falls (with the

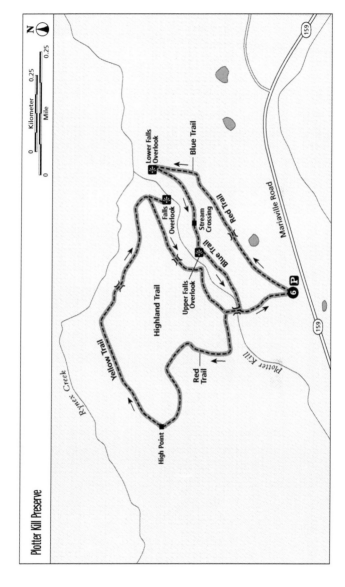

Plotter Kill Preserve

understanding that you will have to return by hiking back up).
If you do walk to the falls, be sure to take the path marked
Entrance (left/southwest) once you come back up the hill.

1.9 There's a little bridge over a wet spot here, followed by a
bridge over a runoff stream that has begun to cut its own
swath in the gorge.

2.0 Take the detour to the left (south) to view the largest waterfall from its very top.

2.1 At this intersection, turn left (southeast) when you see the
Out sign and the arrow.

2.2 You've reached your vehicle at the parking area.

7 Wolf Creek Falls Preserve

This rural meander passes through woods and wetland to a burbling creek, disclosing a series of pleasingly tumbling waterfalls.

Distance: 1.5-mile loop
Approximate hiking time: 1 hour
Difficulty: Easy
Trail surface: Dirt path
Best seasons: Apr through Oct
Other trail users: Joggers, cross-country skiers
Canine compatibility: Dogs permitted on leash
Fees and permits: None
Schedule: Open dawn to dusk

Maps: www.mohawkhudson
.org/preserves/wolf-creek-falls
-preserve
Trailhead facilities: None
Trail contact: Mohawk Hudson Land Conservancy, 425 Kenwood Ave., Delmar, 12054; (518) 436-6346; www.mohawkhudson.org
Special considerations: Insect repellent is highly recommended June through Sept.

Finding the trailhead: From the intersection of I-87 (Northway) and US 20 (Western Avenue) in Albany, go west about 8 miles to NY 146. Turn left (west/toward Altamont) on NY 146 and follow it to a right (north) onto Maple Avenue. Continue north as Maple Avenue becomes Bozenkill Road, and watch for the parking lot on your left (south), just after the house at 774 Bozenkill Rd. **GPS:** N42 43.284' / W74 05.135'.

The Hike

These 135 acres in the town of Knox were the property of a state university professor, Steve Brown, before they became an official preserve under the auspices of the Mohawk Hudson Land Conservancy. We can't thank Dr. Brown enough for saving this little parcel, with its pretty creeks, more than 3.0 miles of trails, abundant wildflowers, and multiple habitats for birds and animals.

The preserve has well-marked trails: the Steven Brown and Patricia (Stocking) Brown Nature Trails. These trails create a network of routes through the preserve's woodlands, providing several access points to the creek and a handful of man-made landmarks to help you maintain your orientation. Stone walls crisscross the preserve, the remains of farmers' property lines between fields and meadows, hearkening to the land's past as a sheep farm. The northeast preserve boundary hosts a railroad track just beyond a patch of wetland—and while no trails approach the tracks, you may hear the roar of a passing engine during your hike. The remains of a stone washing basin and railroad siding are reminders that the Delaware and Hudson Railroad once operated a stone quarry nearby.

With many trails from which to choose, this loop is devised to be long enough to feel like a real hike—albeit over fairly level ground with only a couple hills—while providing an overview of the various habitats you'll encounter on both sides of Bozenkill Road.

Woodland birds make a happy home near Wolf Creek, with black-throated green and black-throated blue warblers singing throughout the late spring and Carolina wrens, house wrens, and rose-breasted grosbeaks easily found. Red-eyed and warbling vireos make themselves known with their constant songs. If you're walking through the woods in late spring and a creature bursts from the woods in a flurry of feathers and tail, bristling and shrieking and racing around crazily, it's probably not a maniacal, bipedal hedgehog—it's a ruffed grouse, desperately trying to lure you away from its nest. My hiking partners and I were thrilled to enjoy this rare, if entirely unnerving, sighting during our June hike at Wolf Creek Falls.

Miles and Directions

0.0 Several trails begin at the parking lot. Take the yellow trail, which begins on the left side of the lot as you face away from Bozenkill Road (looking south). In about 350 feet, the gold trail goes right, while the yellow and red trails continue straight. Stay on the yellow trail (straight/east), and cross a stone wall. Then follow the red trail to the left as it crosses the road. Follow the road until you see a double red blaze on a guardrail—the trail turns left (northwest) into the woods here.

0.2 The blue trail makes a left; continue straight (north) on the red trail, along Wolf Creek. There's a small waterfall to your right. In a few hundred feet, the blue trail rejoins the red trail from the left. An unmarked trail goes straight, while the red trail makes a left. Turn left (northwest) with the red trail.

0.3 The first of two benches is on your left (southwest). The red trail goes right; follow the red trail. Cross a creek on rocks. Another small, stair-step waterfall appears on your left. Just before walking down the bank to cross Wolf Creek, a 40-foot detour to the left will reward you with a view of the beautiful waterfall accentuated by a massive glacial erratic.

0.4 Shortly after you pass the remains of the stone-washing basin and rail siding, the red trail goes left, while a short, purple-blazed connecting trail goes right (northwest). Bear right on the purple trail.

0.5 The white trail begins. Continue straight ahead (northwest) on the white trail.

0.7 The white trail goes right (northwest), while the gold trail goes left (south). Stay right on the white trail, passing a junction with the green trail.

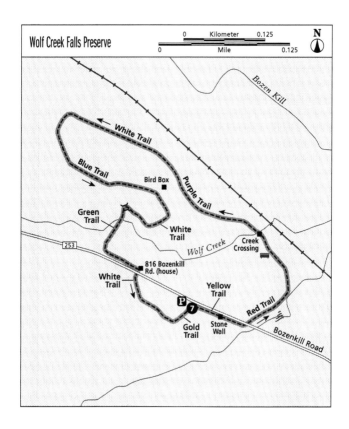

Wolf Creek Falls Preserve

1.0 The blue trail goes left (east), while the white trail goes right (south). Turn left on the blue trail.

1.1 At the junction with the blue and green trails, bear right, then left (south) on the blue trail. In the clearing to your left, you'll see the bird box mentioned on the preserve map. When the white trail crosses the blue trail, turn right (west) on the white trail.

1.2 Pass a bridge over Wolf Creek with a sign that says Private Property—Keep Out. Bear left on the white trail, then make a left (south) on the green trail. There's a bridge over the creek here; you can cross this one: the Musical Bridge. A crude mallet hanging on one of the bridge railing posts will allow you to play simple tunes (such as "London Bridge Is Falling Down") on eight of the bridge planks. Continue straight through a more open area along the property line. At the road, turn left (southeast).

1.4 Pick up the green trail across from the house at 816 Bozenkill Rd. Enter the woods, and go straight on what will become the white trail. Keep following the white trail as it turns left (southeast).

1.5 Turn left (north) on the gold trail, and proceed to the parking area.

8 Christman Sanctuary

A quiet wood disguises a narrow, hidden path along the edge of Bozen Kill, with spectacular views of three waterfalls along its length.

Distance: 2-mile loop
Approximate hiking time: 1 hour
Difficulty: Blue trail is easy, orange trail is moderate
Trail surface: Dirt path
Best seasons: Apr through Oct
Other trail users: Joggers, cross-country skiers
Canine compatibility: No dogs permitted
Fees and permits: None
Schedule: Open dawn to dusk

Maps: *National Geographic Topo!* New York/New Jersey edition
Trailhead facilities: None; do not drink from the kill unless you have purification equipment with you
Trail contact: The Nature Conservancy, 195 New Karner Rd., Albany 12205; (518) 690-7850; www.tnc.org

Finding the trailhead: From Albany, take US 20 (Western Avenue) west toward Duanesburg. Turn left (west) onto Schoharie Turnpike. In about 1.6 miles, watch for the parking area at the top of the hill on your left (south), just after crossing the railroad tracks. **GPS:** N42 44.589' / W74 07.717'.

The Hike

It's no wonder that a number of groups and individuals came together to make Christman Sanctuary the enchanting place that it has become. What a pleasure to explore this little preserve for the first time! You will return to it as often as possible once you've experienced its natural beauty; its ability to inspire contemplation and introspection; and its delightful trails along the Bozen Kill and through cool woods of white pine, cedar, locust, and spruce.

When the Nature Conservancy acquired this property from the Christman family in 1970, the family had long since transformed the land into a nature sanctuary. Will Christman, born on this farm in 1865, began feeding birds in winter in 1888, using the grass and weed seeds he and his wife would find on their property. An award-winning poet in his own right, Christman corresponded with Walt Whitman and Robert Frost, even bringing Frost and his wife to this farm as his guests. Christman's work to maintain his land for its own natural value made him an early role model for land preservation.

Centered on the Bozen Kill, a robust creek that flows with vigor even in midsummer, the sanctuary's greatest attraction is the trail to the lean-to—a side trail that visitors could easily miss, as it begins with passage through a man-made chink between two limestone walls. From here, volunteers have constructed and secured a cable handrail system to make the narrow trail along a ridge as easy as possible to navigate. Stone steps and a well-maintained path provide access to head-on views of a 30-foot waterfall at the end of the path. You are welcome to walk out onto the shale and limestone creek bed, sit on one of the large boulders or a shale ledge, and spend all the time you like enjoying the waterfall, the time-chiseled limestone walls that surround it, and the tenacious hanging gardens that cling to the rugged rock.

From the lean-to trail, you may wish to complete the blue trail loop and return to your vehicle, or continue to explore the sanctuary on the more up-and-down orange trail. Beginning with a bridgeless creek crossing, the orange trail rounds the forest above the creek and falls, providing additional viewpoints from which to enjoy falling water. The hike through the familiar mix of northern hardwoods may offer a chance to see or hear a barred owl or to spot dozens of migrating and nesting bird species in spring. Chipmunks rule the woods here, popping out of holes in the trail and speeding through the underbrush. Other animals you could spot include raccoon, gray squirrel, opossum, or white-tailed deer, all of which make their homes in the sanctuary.

Miles and Directions

0.0 From the parking area, there's only one trailhead. You're on the blue trail as you pass through an area of open grassland and flowering shrubs.

0.2 At the fork in the trail, go right (south). Cross the bridge as you enter the woods. The well-maintained trail is clearly marked; continue to follow the green disks with blue arrows.

0.3 Take the lean-to trail to the right (west).

0.4 When you reach the creek, the waterfall is in front of you. Look right, and go down some stone steps through a break in the limestone. Follow the easy trail (use the guide cable to help steady yourself on the narrow path), and continue down to creek level, where you will reach a 30-foot waterfall. There's a lean-to here. When you're ready, return to the main trail on the same path.

0.5 Continue on the blue trail to the creek and a sign for the orange trail. To begin the orange trail, cross the creek on rocks and slabs of exposed limestone. This may be impass-able in early spring, when snowmelt swells the creek. If that's the case, continue on the blue trail and complete the loop. Otherwise, the crossing is surprisingly easy. Begin following the orange trail (green disks with orange arrows). At the T

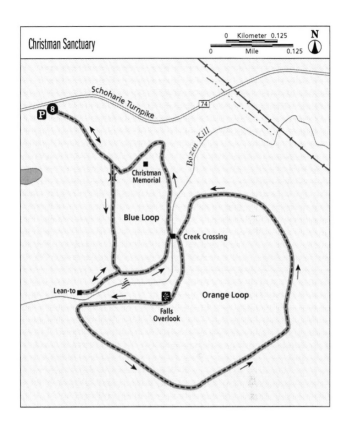

intersection, go right (southwest). Pass through an opening in the stone wall in about 250 feet.

0.7 View the lowest falls from the other side of the creek. Begin a fairly steep incline to reach great views of the other two waterfalls from above.

0.8 From the top of the largest falls, follow the ridge along the creek. Watch for the trail marker—it's parallel to the view of the second waterfall, not the third. Continue around the orange loop through the woods, a fairly conventional hardwood forest with a mix of evergreen and leafy trees. The loop ends as you approach the creek for recrossing.

1.6 Cross the creek and bear right (north) on the blue trail.

1.7 Turn left (southwest) if you'd like to take a short walk to visit the Christman Memorial, a simple plaque in a clearing in the center of the preserve. Otherwise, continue straight on the blue trail.

1.8 You've completed the loop. Turn right (north) to take the trail out of the sanctuary and back to your vehicle.

2.0 Arrive back at the parking area.

9 Taconic Crest Trail to the Snow Hole

Walk a ridgeline in the Taconic Range, with sweeping views of forest-covered hills, to a deep, frigid spot that stays chilled in every season.

Distance: 6.4 miles out and back
Approximate hiking time: 3 hours
Difficulty: More challenging
Trail surface: Dirt path
Best seasons: Mid-May through early Oct
Other trail users: Joggers, trail runners, cross-country skiers
Canine compatibility: Dogs permitted on leash
Fees and permits: None
Schedule: Open dawn to dusk

Maps: Hopkins Memorial Forest, www.williams.edu/CES/hopkins/public/trailmap.htm
Trailhead facilities: None
Trail contact: Williamstown Rural Lands Foundation, Sheep Hill, 671 Cold Spring Rd., Williamstown, MA 01267; (413) 458-2494; https://rurallands.org; or Taconic Hiking Club, https://taconichikingclub.org
Special considerations: Check for deer ticks after your hike.

Finding the trailhead: From Albany, take the New York State Thruway (I-90) east to the junction with I-787 north. Continue on I-787 to exit 7E, and turn east on NY 378 (High Street). At the junction with US 4, turn left (north) and follow US 4 north to the junction with NY 2. Turn right (east) and follow NY 2 for 18.8 miles to Petersburg Pass. Park at the pass and cross the road to find the trailhead—a narrow path up the hill, beginning with a couple hefty steps up on several large rocks. Look for the plastic marker with a white diamond on a blue background. **GPS:** N42 43.468' / W73 16.779'.

The Hike

That special kind of trek that satisfies your body, mind, and spirit, the 35-mile Taconic Crest Trail delivers in the way only a long-distance trail can: Challenging uphill slopes end in long, easy downhill lopes, punctuated by soul-soothing views of endless green hills. Best of all, this 3.2-mile (one way) trail segment has a destination—a compelling crevasse that descends well into the mountain itself, with constant, year-round snow covering its floor.

The trail developed in the 1950s as an outgrowth of a partnership between several public and private agencies, all focused on preserving one of the last nearly unbroken wilderness areas in New York, Massachusetts, and Vermont. Never a highly populated area, the Taconic Mountains nonetheless once served the burgeoning English colonies with a passable route known as the Albany Road, which connected eastern New York State with Deerfield, Massachusetts, in the mid-1700s. Later this road served as an access route for lumbering and maple sugar gathering. As industry gave way to tourism here on the edge of the Berkshire Mountains, the Albany Road faded, and NY 2 became the only road into this area.

The segment described here is predominantly in New York State, crossing into Vermont briefly as it reaches logging roads in the third mile. The ridgeline traverses Hopkins Memorial Forest, a property of Williams College in Massachusetts. This lovely forest is rich in northern hardwoods—sugar maple, yellow birch, and American beech, as well as red maple, eastern hemlock, and black cherry—with concentrated stands of red, white, and chestnut oaks. In the higher elevations you'll find collections of blueberry bushes (picking and eating is permitted) and some huckleberry thickets, both blossoming readily in spring and becoming heavy with fruit in midsummer.

The hike ends at the Snow Hole, a 50-foot-deep chasm in the limestone bedrock just north of the point at which New York, Vermont, and Massachusetts meet. This unusual geological feature maintains a cold enough temperature within its depths to sustain snow and ice at any time of the year. You can climb down into the hole and explore a small cave found close to the top of the hole—but even this small cavern requires some familiarity with caving techniques, so be sure to bring a friend and the equipment you need to explore safely.

You will earn the right to feel good about this hike, as it involves an elevation change of 427 feet over the one-way, 3-mile length. The change is gradual, however, with several inclines that reward you with wonderful views of the surrounding mountains and the valley below.

Miles and Directions

0.0 Park in the lot for Petersburg Pass. There's trail information here, and you'll see trails going off into the mountains to the south. The trail you'll take is across the road to the north. Look for the blue plastic trail marker with a white diamond in the center. Begin with the most challenging part of the trail, climbing up over three large boulders at the trail's base. At the top, proceed on more level ground.

0.2 Pass a display for Hopkins Memorial Forest. Continue to follow the Taconic Crest Trail markers ahead, into the woods. Turn right (north).

0.8 The Shepherd's Well Trail to RRR Brook Trail goes right (east). Continue straight (north).

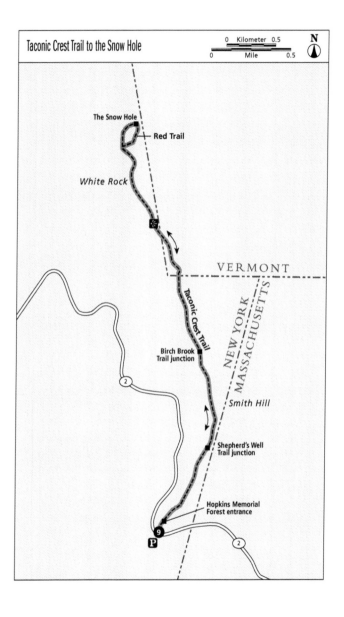

Taconic Crest Trail to the Snow Hole

0   Kilometer   0.5

0   Mile   0.5

N

The Snow Hole — Red Trail

White Rock

VERMONT

Taconic Crest Trail

NEW YORK

MASSACHUSETTS

Birch Brook
Trail junction

Smith Hill

Shepherd's Well
Trail junction

Hopkins Memorial
Forest entrance

9

P

2

2

1.4 The Birch Brook Trail goes right (east). Continue straight (north).

1.9 The nameless trail to the right (east) is a mowed path that wanders through a meadow. Explore if you like, and then continue north on the Taconic Crest Trail.

2.3 Stop to enjoy the great view to the west—this is one of those views that reminds you why you love to hike. You'll find blueberry bushes and other flowering shrubs here.

2.8 A red-blazed trail goes right (northeast). It's the return leg of the trail to the Snow Hole. Continue straight for a little longer.

2.9 A battered wooden sign, facing away from you, once said Snow Hole but has been altered by pranksters. Readable or not, this is the place to turn right (northeast) on the red-blazed trail to see the Snow Hole.

3.2 The red trail takes you to the Snow Hole—look for a deep chasm. This is a nice place to stop, bring out your lunch or gorp, and linger before you begin the trek back. When you're ready, continue around the red loop and rejoin the main trail, turning left (south) for the return.

6.4 Arrive back at the parking area.

10 Vroman's Nose

A quick, steep climb leads to an outstanding view of the Schoharie Valley; bring a picnic lunch and linger at the top.

Distance: 1.8 miles out and back
Approximate hiking time: 1 hour
Difficulty: Moderate
Trail surface: Dirt path
Best seasons: Mid-May through early Oct
Other trail users: Joggers, trail runners
Canine compatibility: Dogs permitted on leash
Fees and permits: None

Schedule: Open dawn to dusk
Map: https://andyarthur.org/map-vromans-nose-unique-area.html
Trailhead facilities: None
Trail contact: Dolores Shaul, Vroman's Nose Preservation Corp., Inc., PO Box 402, Middleburgh, 12122
Special considerations: Be prepared for an elevation change of nearly 500 feet in 0.6 mile.

Finding the trailhead: The trailhead's street address is 192 Mill Valley Rd. in Middleburgh. From Schenectady, take I-88 west to exit 22 (Cobleskill/Middleburgh/NY 7). Turn left at the end of the exit ramp, and follow NY 145 south into Middleburgh. At the junction with NY 30, turn right (southwest) and follow NY 30 to West Middleburgh Road (you'll see the unmistakable cliffs of Vroman's Nose in front of you). Continue west for 0.6 mile on West Middleburgh Road, and watch for the parking area on your left (south). **GPS:** N42 35.680' / W74 21.495'.

The Hike

If you're willing to tough out the 0.5-mile climb to the top of this imposing cliff, your efforts will be well rewarded. From the summit of Vroman's Nose in the town of Fulton, you'll enjoy a 270-degree view of the pastoral Schoharie Valley, from the town of Middleburgh to the northeast to thousands of acres of fertile, cultivated farmland to the north, east, and south—all part of the Schoharie River's alluvial floodplain.

This limestone, shale, and Hamilton sandstone peak, carved out by glaciers as much as 50,000 years ago, underwent a series of transformations as the massive ice sheets melted and deposited sediments. Over thousands of years, the glacial activity isolated this bedrock peak and shaped its striking profile—and when Adam Vroman arrived here in 1713 and established the area's first farm, his name quickly became associated with the landform. Only the most devoted historians will recall Vroman's Land Massacre of 1780—an incident between European-descendant settlers and the area's Iroquois Indians—but members of the Vroman family survived the assault and have continued to live in this valley ever since.

Several trails lead to the summit, but the directions here lead you on the easiest hike to get there. While you can follow a different path back from the summit to create a loop, the other paths are significantly steeper and require some careful hiking during the descent. I recommend returning the way you came, back down the aqua-blazed trail. If you choose to use the blue or yellow trail to return to the parking area, you may find yourself hanging onto trees to slow your progress down the slope. A red-blazed trail leads straight down the eastern wall of the Nose—follow this one at your own risk.

A word about the aqua blazes: You will see this unusual color on several hikes described in this book, and with good reason. These trails are all part of the Long Path, a footpath from Altamont in the Albany area all the way to the George

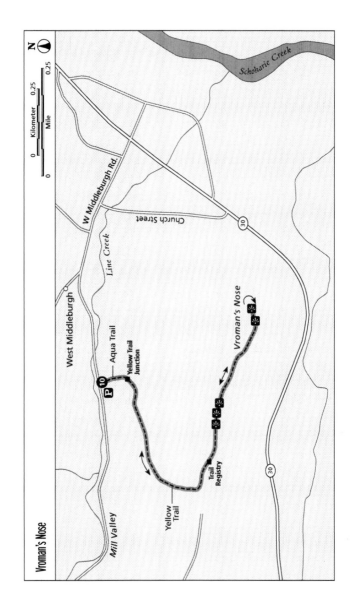

Vroman's Nose

N

Mill Valley

West Middleburgh

W Middleburgh Rd.

Line Creek

Church Street

Schoharie Creek

30

30

P 10

Aqua Trail

Yellow Trail Junction

Yellow Trail

Trail Registry

Vroman's Nose

0   0.25
Kilometer
0   0.25
Mile

Washington Bridge in Fort Lee, New Jersey. Originally a project of the Mohawk Valley Hiking Club back in 1929, this 347-mile trail crosses the Shawangunk and Catskill Mountains, winding through salt marshes at its southern end and climbing to 4,000 feet in the Catskills' boreal forests. Wherever you see this "parakeet aqua" blaze color, you'll know you're on the Long Path. Watch for it in John Boyd Thacher and Mine Kill State Parks.

Miles and Directions

0.0 There's just one trail leading into the woods from the parking area, through the two metal gates. Follow this trail to the point at which two trails diverge, and then follow the aqua blazes up the hill.

0.3 Bear right (west) on the well-worn path. In about 50 feet, the yellow trail goes left (southeast). Go right (west).

0.5 Reach the trail registry. You're nearly at the top of the rise.

0.6 Stop to catch your breath and admire your first great view of the area. Limestone and sandstone outcroppings serve as steps as you climb.

0.7 You're at the top. Congratulations! Continue along the summit of the Nose as the view becomes even broader.

0.8 Arrive at the tip of the Nose. The town slightly to the left (northeast) is Middleburgh; the plowed fields below bear a wide range of vegetables, changing with the seasons—from asparagus in spring to pumpkins, squash, carrots, and parsnips in fall. The orchards you see provide some of New York State's famous apples and other fruits.

0.9 From the top, trails lead down in several directions. The easiest route is to go back the way you came up, especially if you're hiking in winter or early spring, when the path may be snow-covered or wet and slippery.

1.8 You've arrived back at the parking area.

11 Mine Kill State Park

A wide, mellow creek; a placid reservoir; and a young forest make this hilly trail the perfect place to see the seasons change.

Distance: 1.9-mile loop
Approximate hiking time: 1 hour
Difficulty: Moderate
Trail surface: Dirt path
Best seasons: Mid-May through Oct
Other trail users: Joggers, trail runners, cross-country skiers, mountain bikers, snowmobiles
Canine compatibility: Dogs permitted on leash
Fees and permits: A fee is charged per vehicle in season
Schedule: The park is open year-round from dawn to dusk.

Maps: https://parks.ny.gov/documents/parks/MineKillTrail Map.pdf
Trailhead facilities: Restrooms and water are at the reservoir overlook and at the parking area.
Trail contact: Mine Kill State Park, 161 Minekill Rd., North Blenheim 12131; (518) 827-6111; https://parks.ny.gov/parks/minekill/details.aspx
Special considerations: Bow hunting is permitted in fall; wear blaze orange if you hike in Nov and Dec.

Finding the trailhead: The park's street address is 161 Minekill Rd. in North Blenheim. From Albany, take the New York State Thruway (I-90) west to exit 25A (for I-88). On I-88, go west to exit 23 for NY 30 south. Continue south to Middleburgh, where NY 30A becomes NY 30. Go 17 miles south of Middleburgh to reach the park. The entrance is on NY 30, past the New York Power Authority complex. Enter the park and drive east on Minekill Road until it ends at the parking area near the reservoir boat launch. The trailhead is at the entrance to the parking area. **GPS:** N42 26.414' / W74 27.243'.

The Hike

While the main attractions at Mine Kill State Park relate to water—fishing, boating, and swimming in the park's Olympic-size pool—8 miles of trails give hikers the opportunity to enjoy the park's succession forest and breeze-tossed meadows on foot. The hike described here brings you to one of the park's best scenic overlooks, from which you can view the Blenheim-Gilboa Power Project, tucked below Brown Mountain to the east. The power project generates as many as 1 million kilowatts of electricity during peak demand, using Schoharie Creek to create the electricity and returning the creek's water to two reservoirs—the one you see at the park and another one 2,000 feet up at the top of Brown Mountain. Learn more about this unusual power source at www.nypa .gov/power/generation/blenheim-gilboa-pumped-storage.

This entire area is an excellent example of a process environmental scientists call forest succession. As recently as a few decades ago, these woods were farmers' cultivated fields. Plants, shrubs, and trees returned to the land through seeds blown in on the wind, while some seeds were sown by unsuspecting animals, birds, and insects as they carried food or waste into the area. The result is thriving woodland that will be a thick forest in a few more decades, as part of the process of natural succession.

The hike takes you up and down the hilly terrain so typical of the Catskill foothills, providing enough challenge to hold your interest while leading you along ridges and down pleasantly gentle slopes. Parts of this route are labeled with interpretive signs to help you identify the trees, plants, and flowers you see while providing information about the changing nature of the park's wild lands. You may leave with an ability to tell the difference between eastern white pine and eastern hemlock or with a new understanding of power generation and its role in this area's growth and development.

Before you leave the park, drive a little farther south on NY 30 to the road's crossing over Mine Kill Creek. Stop here to see Mine Kill Falls, an 80-foot cascade in the limestone alcove of a narrow gorge. Viewing platforms provide great looks from several angles, and the aqua-blazed Long Path passes by here if you're looking for an additional hiking experience—the path follows the creek and eventually links with the orange trail that's described here.

Miles and Directions

0.0   From the trailhead, follow the red trail. Take the mowed path through the meadow and cross the road.

0.1   Proceed up the hill to the scenic overlook.

0.2   From the scenic overlook you can see the Blenheim-Gilboa Power Project, including the dam that creates this reservoir from Schoharie Creek. There are picnic tables and benches here, as well as restrooms. When you are ready, continue south on the red-blazed path you followed to the viewpoint. (Another red-blazed trail goes south from the restrooms. Both lead in the right direction and connect with the orange trail to the south.)

0.3   Turn right (west) on the orange-blazed trail, and walk downhill to a nice view of the surrounding hills and treetops.

0.4   At the intersection, bear right on the combined red and orange trails.

0.6   The orange trail splits and goes toward some buildings to the right. Continue straight (west).

0.9   The orange trail makes a sharp left and briefly joins the aqua trail (the Long Path). Turn left (east) and continue on the orange trail. From here, much of the path is downhill. Cross

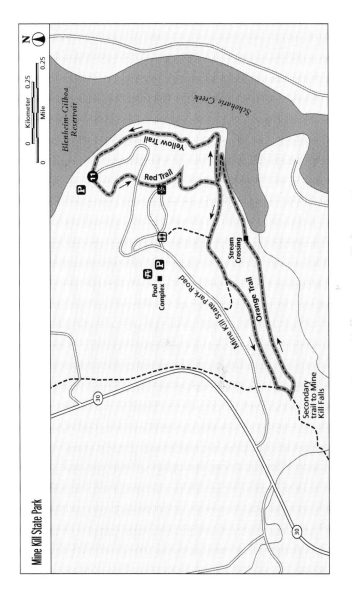

Mine Kill State Park

N

Blenheim-Gilboa Reservoir

Schoharie Creek

Yellow Trail

11

P

Red Trail

Orange Trail

Stream Crossing

Mine Kill State Park Road

Pool Complex

P

Secondary trail to Mine Kill Falls

30

30

0   Kilometer   0.25

0   Mile   0.25

a meadow with tall grasses and wildflowers, and reenter the forest.

1.3   Cross a runoff stream on rocks.

1.5   Bear right on the orange trail. This is where Schoharie Creek and the Blenheim-Gilboa Reservoir join, to your right.

1.6   Bear right (east) on the yellow trail. Alternately, you can rejoin the red trail and return to the overlook. But to complete this loop, follow the yellow trail, which is a bit more hilly and rugged.

1.8   Cross the road and return to the trailhead at the parking area.

1.9   Arrive back at the parking lot.

12 Five Rivers Environmental Education Center

North Loop Trail

This well-tended trail leads along an exquisite meadow, into the woods, and along wetlands for a full range of natural sights.

Distance: 2.1-mile loop
Approximate hiking time: 1.25 hours
Difficulty: Easy
Trail surface: Dirt path
Best seasons: Apr through Oct
Other trail users: Joggers
Canine compatibility: No dogs permitted
Fees and permits: None
Schedule: Grounds are open from sunrise to sunset daily. Visitor center is open weekdays and Sat from 9 a.m. to 4:30 p.m. The visitor center is closed on state and federal holidays.
Maps: www.dec.ny.gov/docs/administration_pdf/5rivermap.pdf
Trailhead facilities: Water and restrooms are in the visitor center.
Trail contact: Five Rivers Environmental Education Center, 56 Game Farm Rd., Delmar 12054; (518) 475-0291; www.dec.ny.gov/education/1835.html

Finding the trailhead: From Albany, take NY 443 southwest to the village of Delmar. Pass through the Elm Avenue traffic light and continue to Orchard Street. Turn right (northwest) on Orchard Street, and then turn left (west) on Game Farm Road. The center is straight ahead. **GPS:** N42 36.624' / W73 53.376'.

The Hike

Originally New York's first state-run experimental game farm, Five Rivers' long legacy of environmental education and stewardship began back in the 1930s, when the Civilian Conservation Corps built facilities for the study of ruffed grouse. Over the ensuing forty years, the game farm advanced to the forefront of environmental research and conservation, and we owe many modern techniques to the successful work completed here.

A walk through the woods can still reveal the easy-to-flush grouse, as well as dozens of other bird species, a plentiful supply of eastern chipmunks and eastern cottontails, the occasional white-tailed deer, and other critters that thrive in this unusual preserve. Listen for eastern bluebird; the "weep, weep" call of the eastern towhee; and a wide variety of warbler species—from yellow and yellow-rumped to Nashville, Tennessee, black-and-white, black-throated green, and black-throated blue. Red-eyed and warbling vireos call from every direction, and scarlet tanagers dart from tree to tree in the thickest parts of the forest.

If you enjoy your walk here, come back for a public program or guided hike, or pick up one of the seasonal interpretive brochures in the visitor center and take on another of the shorter trails at the center. In particular, the 0.5-mile Beaver Tree Trail brings you close to Beaver Pond by wandering through the woods that surround it. The pretty Vlomankill Trail, a 0.75-mile loop, follows the Vloman Kill through a ravine lined with hemlocks and exposed bedrock. Several other trails give you opportunities to learn about the plants, trees, birds, and animals that make this carefully preserved nature center their home.

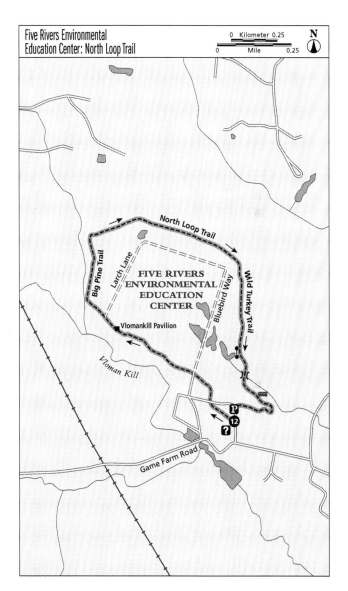

Miles and Directions

0.0 From the parking lot, find the North Loop Trailhead in the northwest corner of the lot. Turn left (west) to begin the trail.

0.1 Cross the road and turn left (northwest) at the intersection for the Old Field Trail. Continue to follow the signs for the North Loop.

0.2 Cross Bluebird Way (road) and continue straight (northwest) on the mowed-grass path.

0.3 Go straight on the road. A grassy path goes left (south).

0.5 Arrive at Vlomankill Pavilion. This is a nice place to stop and have a picnic.

0.6 Turn left (northwest). Larch Lane goes right (northeast).

0.7 The Big Pine Trail goes left (west). Continue straight (north).

0.8 At a junction with the trail to the service road, continue straight (north) through the woods.

1.4 The North Loop Trail turns right (south) and follows the road back to the visitor center. For a more interesting route, pass this junction and turn right (south) at the next one, which is the junction with the Wild Turkey Trail. Walk along a lovely meadow.

1.8 There's a gate here to the right (west), which goes to the Pond Loop. Continue straight (south) along the meadow.

1.9 Cross a bridge over a stream. Bear left (east) with the path, and reach an area with a bench. Go right (west) to return to the parking area.

2.1 You've reached the parking lot and your vehicle.

13 Indian Kill Nature Preserve

A rushing stream, two waterfalls, a quiet wetland, dry uplands, and higher bluffs—this little preserve packs a whole lot of nature into a scant 100 acres.

Distance: 1.7 miles out and back

Approximate hiking time: 1 hour

Difficulty: Easy

Trail surface: Dirt path

Best seasons: Apr through Oct

Other trail users: Cross-country skiers

Canine compatibility: Dogs permitted on leash

Fees and permits: None

Schedule: Open daily dawn to dusk

Maps: https://nnywaterfalls .com/indiankill/indiankillthird falls/Indian_Kill%20Brochure.pdf

Trailhead facilities: None

Trail contact: Schenectady County Economic Development and Planning Department, 107 Nott Ter., Schaffer Heights Ste. 303, Schenectady 12308; (518) 386-2225; https://schenectady-countyny.gov/ed-planning

Special considerations: A creek crossing on rocks is required; wear waterproof shoes or amphibious footwear (reef runners).

Finding the trailhead: From Schenectady take NY 50 north to Glenridge Road, and turn right (east). Continue 1.3 miles on Glenridge Road to Maple Avenue. Turn left (north) on Maple Avenue and go 0.4 mile to the parking lot, which is about 0.1 mile after the junction of Maple Avenue and Hetcheltown Road. The trailhead is in the parking area. **GPS:** N42 52.293' / W73 54.403'.

The Hike

In the heart of a populated area about 12 minutes north of the city of Schenectady, this little 100-acre preserve offers a natural respite from the surrounding suburbs along the banks of the rambling Indian Kill.

You will recognize the native hardwoods that thrive in this area on the edge of the north country: The ubiquitous maple trees are joined by hickory, cherry, and oak, while the understory supplies excellent habitat for a healthy eleven fern species. Conifer plantations of cedar, hemlock, and pine grace the hillsides, while fertile wetlands lay in the preserve's lowest areas.

Come in spring for the wildflower show, a celebration of trillium, jack-in-the-pulpit, hepatica, mayapple, marsh marigold, cohosh, and many others. Even in midsummer, when the blooms have faded, layers of ferns cover the forest floor and edge the wetlands, lending their jade and emerald shades to the scene.

The Claire Schmitt Trail works its way from one end of the preserve to the other, requiring a creek crossing at Third Falls (which is actually the first natural waterfall you will see). In summer and fall, this is a simple crossing on exposed rock; from March until late June, however, the rushing creek and wet, slippery shale and limestone make this a dicey choice. The creek is deep enough in places between the rock faces that it will submerge your hiking boots. The Miles and Directions turn back at this point, but if you can get across with ease, the red trail continues for another 0.5 miles to Second Falls. Adding this segment will lengthen your hike by a total of 1 mile, making the entire hike 2.7 miles long.

Miles and Directions

0.0 From the parking area, there's just one trailhead. Proceed up the red trail to the dam.

0.2 Cross the little dam on the bridge. Bear right (north) along the creek, and start up the switchbacks.

0.3 At the top of the switchbacks, the yellow trail goes right, as does the red trail. Turn right (north) and follow the red blazes.

0.5 Through the trees, there's a nice view of the land below. An unmarked trail leads down (north) from here. Turn left (west) and stay on the red trail.

0.6 At the top of the gradual incline, turn right (north) on the red trail. An unmarked trail goes left. In a few feet, the red trail goes right, while yellow goes left. Go right (north) on the red trail.

0.7 The red trail goes left (west) and down the steps to the creek side. An unmarked trail goes straight. Follow the red trail down the steps.

0.8 Cross a small bridge over a feeder stream, then cross a larger bridge about ten steps later. After the larger bridge, turn left on the red trail. The yellow trail goes off to the left; continue straight (north) on the red trail.

0.9 Bear right, down to the creek side and Third Falls. The trail continues across the creek for another 0.5 mile to Second Falls. If you can get across the creek, continue to follow the red trail (the only trail from this point forward). When you reach Second Falls, turn around and come back to this point. If you're not making the crossing, this is the turnaround point for the return hike. Follow the yellow trail back to the dam.

1.1 Bear right (south) on the yellow trail. Cross a crevasse made by a stream—the faint beginning of a ravine that will take shape over the next several thousand years. Then cross a series of three small bridges over other streams.

Indian Kill Nature Preserve

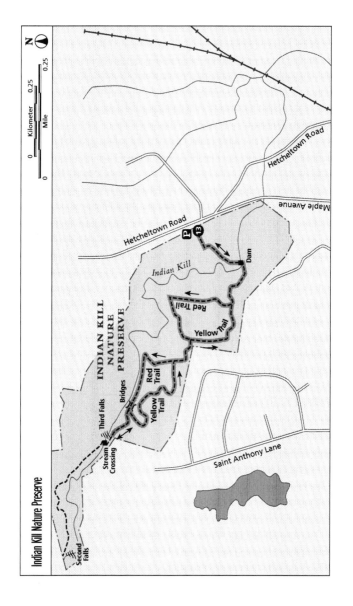

1.2 Continue to bear right (southeast) on the yellow trail at this junction with the red trail.

1.4 Leave the yellow trail and go straight ahead (east) on the red trail, down the switchbacks to the dam.

1.7 Cross the dam and arrive back at the parking area.

14 Schodack Island State Park

Walk in the footsteps of native people who lived here 4,000 years ago on this slender island between the Hudson River and Schodack Creek.

Distance: 5.1-mile loop, including 0.6-mile out-and-back spur
Approximate hiking time: 2.5 hours
Difficulty: Moderate
Trail surface: Dirt path
Best seasons: Apr through Oct
Other trail users: Trail runners, cross-country skiers, snowshoers
Canine compatibility: Dogs permitted on leash, must have poof of vaccines
Fees and permits: A fee is charged per vehicle on weekends and holidays from early May to mid-October. All other times are free.

Schedule: Open daily, dawn to dusk
Maps: https://parks.ny.gov/parks/schodackisland/
Trailhead facilities: Restrooms and water are in the developed area near the trailhead.
Trail contact: Schodack Island State Park, 1 Schodack Way, Schodack Landing 12156; (518) 732-0187; https://parks.ny.gov/parks/schodackisland/
Special considerations: Wear orange during hunting seasons (Oct–Feb).

Finding the trailhead: From I-787 in Albany, take US 20 east and cross the Hudson River. Continue to NY 9J. Follow NY 9J south approximately 8 miles, past Castleton-on-Hudson. Watch for the large sign for the park entrance on the right (west). Drive into the area with the pavilion, playground, and boat launch. The trailhead is in the southwest corner of the parking area. **GPS:** N42 29.918' / W73 46.571'.

The Hike

Imagine the seafaring life of English explorer Henry Hudson, who sailed on the ship *Half Moon* in 1609 on behalf of the Dutch United East India Company to find a passage to the exotic lands to the east. In midvoyage, the waters in Europe's northern seas became too treacherous, and Hudson made the kind of independent call that signifies a great captain: He turned west and sailed for the New World, eventually finding the mouth of the river that one day would bear his name. Here, on the northern end of Schodack Island, Hudson claimed this land for Holland.

Ever reasonable in their commercial pursuits, the Dutch agreed to an equitable arrangement with the Mohican people who lived on the island, purchasing the upper island from them in 1650, while the Mohicans continued to live in the lower portion. Dredging operations in the 1920s covered the remains of the Mohican village, but the rest of the island has returned to the way it probably looked back when Hudson and his sailors made landfall. Today, you can enjoy this wilderness on an easy, level hike, which I've rated "moderate" only because of its considerable length.

On a slim island flanked by a major river and a wide creek, you are entitled to expect excellent views of flowing water and the mainland beyond—and while you can glimpse the Hudson through the trees as you walk, broader views are only visible during the leafless season from late November through March. A spur trail on the return leg brings hikers to the edge of Schodack Creek, where a picnic table provides a resting place as you take in the serene surroundings. Happily, three seasons of the year bring vibrant colors to the island landscape, with wildflowers lining the trail, including oxeye daisy, mullein, Queen Anne's lace, Joe Pye weed, daisy fleabane, and long-leafed speedwell. In fall, the northern forest turns amber and crimson as oak, maple, beech, and aspen transform for your viewing enjoyment, before tossing off their leaves and revealing the river and creek that edge the island.

Miles and Directions

0.0 Begin walking from the trailhead in the southwest corner of the parking area. There's just one trail heading south.

0.6 A trail goes off to the left; it connects with the return leg of the loop. Continue straight. From here, you enter an area where hunting with firearms is allowed in season; wear blaze orange if you're hiking October through February. You'll spot occasional orange plastic disks that serve as trail markers in state parks; these are infrequent on this hike, but you won't go wrong if you just continue straight (south).

1.0 The trail forks. Take the right (south) fork with red trail markers. (The left fork crosses the island to the return leg of the loop.)

1.8 A trail goes left, crossing the island. Continue straight (south).

2.1 You've reached the turnaround point in the loop. A sign here notes that if you continue straight, the trail is subject to tidal flooding and muddy conditions during wet seasons and high tides. It's a long way—more than 2 miles—to the end of the island and a possible water view, so turn left (east) and begin the return trek. Yellow plastic trail markers are visible on the trail to the left.

2.5 Bear right (north) at the fork in the trail, following the red markers (a connector trail goes left).

2.8 Cross a small bridge over a wet area.

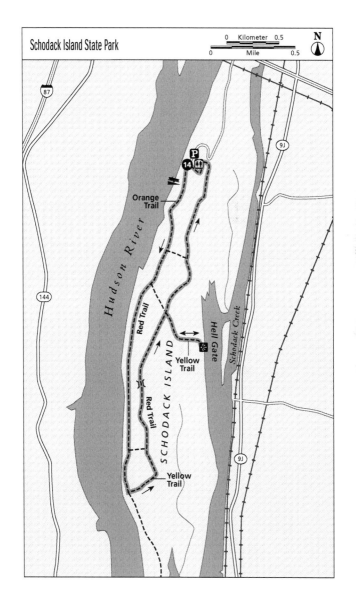

Schodack Island State Park

3.4 A connector trail goes left (west). To your right (east), a trail spur marked in yellow leads to a fine view of Schodack Creek, the best water view you'll find on this hike. Turn right.

3.7 The spur trail ends at Schodack Creek. There's a picnic table here, making this a good place to pause before completing the loop. When you're ready, follow the spur back to the main trail, and turn right (north).

4.4 A connector trail goes left. Continue straight (north), following the yellow markers.

5.0 The park's maintenance area is to your right (east). A gravel path goes left (west) to the developed area of the park. Turn left. When you reach the mowed area, the pavilion is to your right, while restrooms are ahead on your left. Turn left on the gravel path to return to the parking area.

5.1 Arrive back at the parking lot and your vehicle.

15 Lewis A. Swyer Preserve

In the mood for something exotic? This boardwalk ramble takes you to a freshwater marsh and swamp that surround you with tall vegetation.

Distance: 1.2 miles out and back

Approximate hiking time: 45 minutes

Difficulty: Easy

Trail surface: Boardwalk

Best seasons: Apr through Nov

Other trail users: Hikers only

Canine compatibility: Pets not permitted

Fees and permits: Free

Schedule: Open daily dawn to dusk

Maps: https://www.nature.org/ content/dam/tnc/nature/en/ documents/swyer-preserve-map .pdf

Trailhead facilities: None

Trail contact: The Nature Conservancy, 195 New Karner Rd., Ste. 200, Albany 12205; (518) 456-0655; www.nature .org/en-us/get-involved/how -to-help/places-we-protect/ eastern-lewis-a-swyer-preserve/

Special considerations: Insect repellent is a must.

Finding the trailhead: From I-787 in Albany, take US 9 and 20 to Rensselaer. Turn right on NY 9J and continue 7.7 miles through Castleton. Watch for the preserve's small parking area along the road to the right (west side), about a half-mile after you go under a railroad pass. The trailhead is about 500 feet south of the parking area as you reach Mill Creek. From the south, take NY 9J north, and pass through the flashing light in Stuyvesant Landing. The parking area is 2 miles north of the flashing light. **GPS:** N42 25.072' / W73 46.147'.

The Hike

You may live in the Capital Region your entire life without coming upon Mill Creek, a quiet tributary that penetrates the Hudson River's eastern bank near Stuyvesant Landing. Here at the edge of the Hudson, Mill Creek enjoys the ebb and flow of the tide—yes, the Atlantic Ocean's tide some 150 miles south. Saltwater does not find its way this far upriver, however, so Mill Creek and its surroundings have formed a freshwater marsh and swamp, a place where water flows in and out, covering the submerged land with nutrients that propagate a distinctive and verdant ecosystem.

The preserve, acquired by the Nature Conservancy in 1989, formed as a result of river dredging, a process of lowering the river floor to keep the waterway deep enough for major shipping traffic. The material dredged from the riverbed ended up here, creating land at the mouth of the creek. Today the Swyer Preserve protects one of only five freshwater tidal swamps in New York State.

Here the vegetation includes tall spires of pickerelweed, which bear bright purple towers of blooms in summer. The broad leaves of arrow arum sprout from the waterlogged earth. Rice cutgrass and swamp milkweed spread their roots in the marshy land, while ash, maple, slippery elm, and oak trees shade the creek's banks and provide homes for yellow warblers, warbling vireos, gray catbirds, veeries, and wood thrushes. Watch for common yellowthroat, Virginia rail, green heron, and red-winged blackbirds among the tall grasses, and keep an eye out for snapping turtles or even a water snake.

The short, pleasant boardwalk offers many open viewing points, with a tower at the end that provides a terrific view

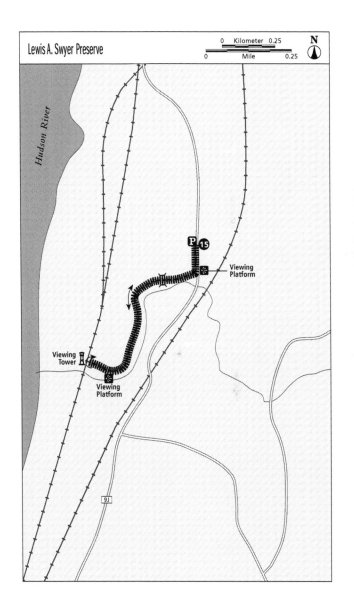

Lewis A. Swyer Preserve

Hudson River

Viewing Platform

Viewing Tower

Viewing Platform

P 15

9J

of the river and the passing trains on its west bank. When the tides are particularly high in spring, the water brings silt and mud up and over the boardwalk, so wear shoes that provide a good grip on a wet, slippery surface.

Miles and Directions

0.0 Park here and walk south 500 feet to the trailhead.

0.2 At the preserve sign, turn right onto the boardwalk. Stop at the kiosk, where you'll find tide tables and other useful information. In a few steps you'll come to a viewing platform, which provides a long view of the creek. Note all the large, broad-leaved vegetation here. Shortly you'll cross a bridge.

0.6 Here is another platform, with an open view of the creek and surrounding woods. There are benches here. Watch for snails, listen for spring peepers in April and May, and see if you can hear or spot a pileated woodpecker. Just around the next bend, the boardwalk ends at a viewing tower. It's nineteen steps to the top. When you're ready, retrace your steps to return to the parking area.

1.2 You've emerged from the trail and are back at your vehicle.

16 Peebles Island State Park

Spacious water views surround this island where the Mohawk and Hudson Rivers meet, popping up from every angle as you walk the perimeter trail.

Distance: 2-mile loop
Approximate hiking time: 1 hour
Difficulty: Easy
Trail surface: Dirt and mowed-grass path
Best seasons: Apr through Oct
Other trail users: Trail runners, cross-country skiers
Canine compatibility: Dogs permitted on leash
Fees and permits: Free
Schedule: Open daily, sunrise to sunset

Maps: https://parks.ny.gov/documents/parks/PeeblesIslandTrailMap.pdf
Trailhead facilities: Restrooms, water, and information are available in the visitor center.
Trail contact: Peebles Island State Park, 1 Delaware Ave. North, Cohoes, 12047; (518) 268-2188; https://parks.ny.gov/parks/peeblesisland/details.aspx

Finding the trailhead: From I-90 in Albany, take exit 6A (I-787 north) to Cohoes. Continue on I-787 as it becomes NY 787. At the fourth traffic light, turn right (east) onto Ontario Street (NY 470). Just before the Hudson River bridge to Troy, turn left (north) on Delaware Avenue. The bridge to Peebles Island is at the end of Delaware Avenue. Park at the north end of the parking lot, past the Bleachery Complex. The trail begins on a crushed-gravel path. **GPS:** N42 47.098' / W73 40.852'.

The Hike

Steeped in industrial history but most popular for its terrific views of the Mohawk and Hudson Rivers, Peebles Island is a favorite hiking ground for residents of Troy and the smaller towns north of Albany. It's no wonder that this place draws visitors at any time of day and in every season: A wilderness on the edge of a formerly major manufacturing district, the island offers 191 acres of respite from the largely commercialized areas that surround it.

You won't be able to miss the former Cluett, Peabody & Company Powerhouse as you enter the park. Now serving as the park's visitor center, as well as the headquarters for the Erie Canalway National Heritage Corridor, this turn-of-the-twentieth-century edifice housed the Bleachery Complex for the company that supplied manufacturing services to Arrow Shirt Company. Cluett, Peabody & Company was the principal maker of the famous Arrow collars—detachable shirt collars that became iconic as a wardrobe staple for the common man in the 1910s and 1920s. Brilliant advertising turned Cluett, Peabody into the most successful company in the United States in the 1920s, turning out 4 million collars a week. The company continued to function here until 1972; you can learn more by visiting the building and seeing the extensive interpretive displays in the visitor center.

The Bleachery quickly disappears as you begin the hike. In just a few steps, the trail through dense woods leads you to high bluffs over the Mohawk River, where the town of Waterford is visible just across the water. As the path continues, a series of islands come into view: Bock, Goat, and Second Island appear on the west side of Peebles Island, along with one of the many dams built to prevent major flooding during central New York's wet seasons.

At the south end of the island, you can view the split the island forms in the river; rocky shoals appear as you walk north on the island's east side. The uneven, sedimentary-rock-strewn riverbed creates a stretch of rushing whitewater here in late winter and spring.

Miles and Directions

0.0 From the parking area, walk west on the crushed-gravel path. Watch for groundhogs living in the generous understory as you approach the woods and for deer in just about any area along the trail.

0.2 Bear right (north) at the fork in the trail, and enter Oak Grove. Continue to bear right as the trail splinters twice more.

0.3 A side path goes to the right (north). Take this path to reach a great view of the river; it will rejoin the main path shortly.

0.5 This point on the island provides the first wide-open view of the water. Enjoy the vista, then rejoin the main trail and continue straight (south). You can see the town of Waterford across the river, and Bock Island is coming into view further ahead on the right (east).

0.6 A trail marked with red plastic disks goes left (southeast). There's a little pavilion here. Continue straight (south), and bear right ahead for another terrific view of the river. The dam is past Bock Island (south), and the island is now straight ahead when you face the water. Goat Island is past the dam.

0.7 You're now parallel to the dam. Second Island is coming into view.

1.2 Continue straight (south) on the yellow trail. The red trail goes left (north). You're now rounding the southernmost part of the island.

1.3 A rocky area in the river creates a short falling-water phenomenon, with accompanying rapids.

1.4 The yellow trail goes left (north), while the red goes right (northeast). Take the red trail to stay on the island's perimeter.

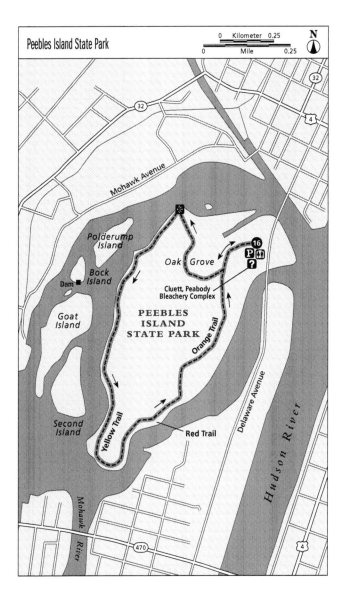

1.7 Turn right (northeast) on the mowed-grass path. (The red trail continues left.) Enter the woods.

1.8 Turn left (north) on the orange-marked trail. Emerge in a meadow that sports tall grasses and leafy plants in summer. Continue straight (north) as you reach the paved area, and cross behind the Bleachery Complex to return to the parking lot.

2.0 You've completed the loop and arrived back at your vehicle.

17 Saratoga National Historical Park

Wilkinson National Recreation Trail

Rolling fields, robust forests, and a dash of history—this hike tours the Revolutionary War battlefield in Saratoga while passing wildflower-rich meadows and bushes laden with berries.

Distance: 4.2-mile loop
Approximate hiking time: 2.25 hours
Difficulty: Moderate
Trail surface: Dirt and mowed-grass path
Best seasons: Apr through Oct
Other trail users: Trail runners, cross-country skiers. You may see horses on connecting trails.
Canine compatibility: Dogs permitted on leash
Fees and permits: Free
Schedule: Open daily to foot traffic from sunrise to sunset. The tour road is open April 1 to November 30 beginning at 9 a.m. The park closes at 7 p.m. from April 1 to September 30, at 5 p.m. from October 1 through the end of daylight saving time, and at 4 p.m. from the beginning

of local standard time through November 30. The tour road is closed December through March, but you may walk the trail in winter. The visitor center is open from 9 a.m. to 5 p.m. daily.
Maps: www.nps.gov/sara/plan yourvisit/maps.htm/; also available at the park visitor center
Trailhead facilities: Restrooms, water, and information are in the visitor center.
Trail contact: Saratoga National Historical Park, 648 Rte. 32, Stillwater 12170; (518) 670-2895; www.nps.gov/sara
Special considerations: Pick up an interpretive trail brochure at the visitor center, and follow the battle's progress as you arrive at each tour stop.

Finding the trailhead: From Albany, take I-87 (Northway) to exit 12. Turn right from the exit ramp onto NY 67 east, and stay to the right as you go through the traffic circle. After the circle, bear left as you enter the next traffic circle, and take the exit for US 9 north (on your right). Continue 1.6 miles to the second traffic light, and turn right (east) on NY 9P. Drive 4.5 miles along Saratoga Lake, and turn right (east) onto NY 423. Continue 5.5 miles to NY 32, and turn right (east) into Saratoga National Historical Park. Park in the main lot, which is located below the visitor center. The trail begins at the back door of the visitor center. **GPS:** N43 00.723' / W73 38.932'.

The Hike

Do you hear the fifes and drums? On this ground in 1777, two battles pitted the well-organized, highly trained British regulars against a compact, fiercely determined army of the newly created United States of America and signaled a sea change in the war for American independence. What the British considered a shallow rebellion turned into a worldwide conflict—and while fighting continued for another six years, the Americans gained an advantage at Saratoga that would eventually result in a new nation conceived in liberty.

Lieutenant William Wilkinson, a British officer, mapped this route during the battle as his troops and others marched through these fields and over the hills. Thanks to his efforts, we can now truly walk in the footsteps of the opposition forces and see the landscape much as they saw it, from their ascent out of the Great Ravine to their defensive positions in the congested woods.

The former fields of the McBride and Freeman farms, which gave up their harvest in 1777 to soldiers on both sides of the conflict, are now overseen by the National Park Service and are similar to the way they appeared during the eighteenth century, although crops are no longer planted here. The Wilkinson National Recreation Trail explores the northern section of Saratoga National Historical Park, linking several places with the park's driving tour road and its interpretive displays.

If you learned all you needed to know about the Revolutionary War in high school, you'll still find plenty to enjoy on this trail—opportunities for bird and butterfly identification abound, and many wildflower varieties bloom here throughout the spring and summer. In fall, when the fields turn gold and violet as they fill with goldenrod and purple aster, the hardwood forests offer multihued landscapes of scarlet, topaz, and aubergine as their leaves succumb to autumn.

Miles and Directions

0.0 Begin at the visitor center. Walk out the back door of the center and follow the footpath to the kiosk that signals the trailhead.

0.3 Bear left (east) on the grassy trail at Station A. Follow the brown signs that say Wilkinson Trail in white print. In spring and summer, look for sensitive fern, black-eyed Susan, goldenrod, Joe Pye weed, common yarrow, and several species of milkweed (including the striking orange variety) in the meadow.

0.5 This trail crosses the park's H (Horse) trail. Continue straight.

0.6 A side trail leads to interpretive material about Breymann Redoubt, a British fortification built by loyalist, German, and Canadian troops. The stop is optional but recommended for its interesting historical content. When you're ready, return to the Wilkinson Trail and continue to the left (south).

0.8 Bear left (southeast) as the loop begins at the tour's Station C.

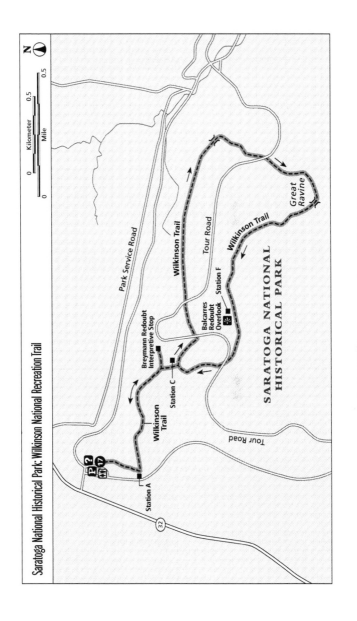

Saratoga National Historical Park: Wilkinson National Recreation Trail

1.1 Cross the tour road and enter a mixed wood of pine and scrub oak. There are lots of berry bushes here and in many places along the trail; look for blackberries and black raspberries, which ripen in late July. Berry eating is permitted in the park.

1.2 The Liaison Trail goes right (south). Continue straight (east).

1.3 Cross the road and continue straight.

1.9 Cross the ST trail. There's a bridge over a stream as you reach Station F. Continue straight and to the right (south), and enter an open field of ferns and emerging aspen. This area was farmland during the war, supplying the British troops with fresh produce to forage as they waited for the next skirmish with the Americans.

2.1 Cross the road. You'll see many wild blackberry bushes along the trail. Enter the woods and cross a ditch in which the British waited for 2 weeks for reinforcements that never arrived. In a few steps, begin the descent into the Great Ravine.

2.4 At the bottom of the long, gradual, downward slope, cross a bridge over a stream. Begin the ascent out of the ravine—an elevation increase of about 120 feet.

3.1 Cross the paved trail, and continue straight (northwest).

3.2 Cross the paved trail again, and continue straight (northwest). You're heading in the direction of the visitor center, as signs indicate.

3.3 Cross the road, and bear left (north) onto the trail. Watch and listen for eastern bluebirds, bobolinks, and field sparrows in these fields.

3.5 You've completed the loop. Turn left (northwest) and head back toward the visitor center. The trail inclines gradually for the last 0.7 mile to the trailhead and visitor center.

4.2 Arrive back at the trailhead.

18 Grafton Lakes State Park

Long Pond Trail

This rocky ramble offers surprising challenges as it circles a pretty pond on relatively flat terrain.

Distance: 2.6-mile loop

Approximate hiking time: 1.5 hours

Difficulty: Moderate

Trail surface: Boulder-rich dirt path

Best seasons: Apr through Oct

Other trail users: Cross-country skiers, ice skaters, and snowshoe hikers in winter; swimmers at the beach area, fishermen at the north-end parking area

Canine compatibility: Dogs permitted on leash

Fees and permits: A fee is charged per vehicle from Memorial Day to Labor Day; the fee is higher when the swimming beach is open. The fee is charged on weekends only from Labor Day to Columbus Day.

Schedule: Open daily, 8 a.m. to dusk

Maps: www.avenzamaps.com/maps/101556

Trailhead facilities: Restrooms and refreshments are at the beach.

Trail contact: Grafton Lakes State Park, 254 Grafton Lakes State Park Way, Grafton 12082; (518) 279-1155; https://parks.ny.gov/parks/graftonlakes

Special considerations: Wear shoes with ankle support for hiking on and around boulders embedded in the trail.

Finding the trailhead: From Albany, take I-787 (Northway) to exit 9E for NY 7 (east). Bear right (east) onto NY 7 and continue to NY 278. Bear right (southeast) on NY 278 and continue 1.5 miles to NY 2. Turn left (east) on NY 2 and continue 7.6 miles to the park entrance, on the left (north) on North Long Pond Road. Begin the hike at the beach at Long Pond. **GPS:** N42 46.985' / W73 27.044'.

The Hike

Here on a ridge above the Hudson River Valley and the Taconic River, the 2,357-acre Grafton Lakes State Park provides swaths of rugged forests and five natural ponds. This multiuse recreational area offers its fields, streams, woods, and lakes for all manner of outdoor activities, from horseback riding to nature photography, as well as excellent fishing for a number of northeastern species, including pickerel, bass, and perch. Of the 25 miles of trails that pass through the park, the Long Pond Trail rises to the top of the list, a level but surprisingly challenging hike because of the wide beds of boulders that make for rocky passage along the otherwise easy route.

A forest of characteristic northern hardwoods lines Long Pond on all sides, shading a thriving understory that fills with wildflowers in spring and summer, as well as a wide variety of woodland bird species. On the forest floor, look for painted and red trillium, Canada mayflower, and mayapple in May; wild geranium in early June; and species like wild sarsaparilla, trout lily, foamflower, and starflower in summer. Listen for yellow, black-throated blue, and black-throated green warblers; white-throated and white-crowned sparrows; wood thrush; and ovenbird during the spring migration, as well as the ubiquitous blue jays, mockingbirds, northern flickers, and downy and hairy woodpeckers that make the forest their year-round home. Over the water, you'll see tree and bank swallows darting this way and that, catching mosquitoes in midair.

As oak, maple, and beech give way to white pine and hemlock, the forest floor becomes a carpet of aromatic needles that hamper additional vegetation. Here you can see

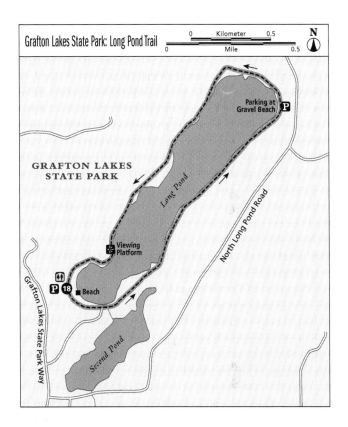

GRAFTON LAKES STATE PARK

well into the forest—so watch for chipmunks, white-tailed deer, eastern cottontail rabbits, and groundhogs that may seek shelter here. Gray squirrels chatter from behind trees and overhead, and red fox sightings are sometimes reported. Toward dusk, watch for raccoons emerging from their dens in some concealed hideaway.

Miles and Directions

0.0   Begin just northeast of the beach. Follow the cement walk around to the right until you reach the trailhead.

0.2   Arrive at the trailhead proper. Follow the round, red disk markers that begin at the boat rental, just before the trail-head. As you walk up the dirt path, you will see signs that warn of more difficult hiking. These are areas in which many large rocks are embedded in the soil. Most are flat and easy to walk over, but you will need to watch the placement of your feet as you hike. After the first stretch of boulder-heavy surface, the well-worn path follows the edge of the lake just inside the deliciously shady woods.

1.2   Reach the northeastern end of the pond, where there's a gravel beach and parking area. You may see some people fishing here. The trail continues straight ahead, across the parking area and a little to the right.

2.4   As you come back down the western side of the pond, you reach a viewing platform that extends out into the pond past the forest fringe. This spot offers the best pond view on the entire hike, giving you a sense of what the area looked like when the Mohican people lived here in the 1600s and well before.

2.5   The dirt trail ends at the beginning of the cement walkway around the beach. Return to the parking area by way of the walkway.

2.6   Arrive back at the parking area and your vehicle.

Clubs and Trail Groups

Adirondack Mountain Club, Albany Chapter, 959 US-9, Queensbury 12804; (518) 668-4447; https://albany.adk .org. The club offers a variety of hikes and programs to share the joy and knowledge of outdoor recreation.

Audubon Society of the Capital Region, Stuyvesant Plaza, PO Box 38177, Albany 12203; www.capitalregionaudu-bon.org. The Capital chapter of the Audubon Society conserves and protects birds and wildlife habitat through advocacy and education. It offers field trips, sanctuary management, and environmental education.

Hudson-Mohawk Bird Club, c/o Five Rivers Environmental Education Center, 56 Game Farm Rd., Delmar 12054; (518) 439-8080; www.hmbc.net. The club is devoted to field birding and the appreciation of wild birds through monthly programs, field trips, and its sanctuary in Schenectady.

Long Path North Hiking Club; PO Box 855, Schoharie 12157; (518) 944-7734; www.Schoharie-conservation .org/memberclubs/lpn/index.html. Formed as an off-shoot of the New York/New Jersey Trail Conference, this organization constructs and maintains the Long Path and offers hikes on the trail in every season.

Taconic Hiking Club, https://taconichikingclub.org. For people interested in nature study, hiking, backpacking, camping, cycling, canoeing, kayaking, snowshoeing, cross-country skiing, and more.

About the Author

Randi Minetor has written more than fifty books for imprints of Rowman & Littlefield, including *Hiking Waterfalls New York* (three editions); *Hiking through History New York*; *Hiking the Lower Hudson River Valley*; *Hiking the Catskills* with co-author Stacey Freed; and *Best Easy Day Hikes* guides to Rochester, Buffalo, Syracuse, Albany, and the Hudson River Valley. She is also the author of *Birding New England*, *Birding Florida*, and *Birding Texas* for Falcon Guides, and she has written seven books in the nonfiction Death in the National Parks series for Lyons Press. She and her husband, photographer Nic Minetor, live in Rochester.